Proud Traditions and Future Challenges

Proud Traditions and Future Challenges— The University of Wisconsin–Madison Celebrates 150 Years

. . .

Edited by David Ward
Chancellor
University of Wisconsin–Madison
Co-edited by Noel Radomski

Published for the Office of the Chancellor
by the Office of University Publications
University of Wisconsin-Madison, 1999

Publication of this book was made possible by funding
from the University of Wisconsin Foundation.

ISBN 0-9658834-2-6

Distributed by the University of Wisconsin Press
Madison, Wisconsin
www.wisc.edu/wisconsinpress/

Contents

Preface

THE UNIVERSITY OF WISCONSIN–MADISON sesquicentennial provides numerous opportunities to reflect on our distinguished history of education, research, and service. The 150th anniversary is also a time to look ahead and create a vision for strengthening the university's partnership with the state.

During the university's jubilee, my predecessor also reflected on those same issues. In 1904, during the university's fiftieth anniversary, President Van Hise consolidated many of the components of the great research university we have today. Now it is our responsibility to help shape the future during a period of great change within our country and institutions of higher education. I am excited by the opportunity the sesquicentennial affords us as we begin the journey into the next millennium.

This publication brings together seven essays to help advance the dialogue on the future of our great state university. The essays, written by academic staff and faculty, examine current and future challenges confronting the UW–Madison. Some essays offer predictions of the future, and several essays pose fundamental questions about the university's future. What follows is a brief review of the contents of this volume.

In chapter 1, "The Challenges of Irreversible Change in Higher Education: The University of Wisconsin–Madison in the 1990s," I provide an overview of historical change in higher education in general, and the significant internal and external challenges confronting the UW–Madison in particular. The essay concludes with strategies for maintaining the UW–Madison's preeminence in the twenty-first century.

Chapter 2, "The Future of the Liberal Arts," by Dean Phillip R. Certain, consists of five sections. The first section examines the origins and evolution of the liberal arts within higher education and at the UW–Madison. The second section describes the recent challenge of creating a sense of community within a complex research university. The third section looks at the liberal arts challenge for the search for truth, which may conflict with elements of today's prevailing views. The fourth section discusses the tension between the theory and application of academic freedom. And finally, section five discusses the role of the liberal arts within a land-grant institution with strong and competing professional schools. A concluding series of questions guide the reexamination of the liberal arts.

The third chapter, "Using Technology Wisely: New Approaches to Teaching and Learning through Technology," by Kathleen Christoph, begins with an overview of recent approaches to teaching and learning through technology at the UW–Madison and describes new tools that can expand the learning community. The chapter also reviews how uses of technology present new challenges in the areas of faculty and instructional staff support, rewards, and intellectual property ownership. The chapter also raises questions about the future of higher education within an intensive competitive marketplace. The chapter concludes by discussing current UW–Madison responses and directions in using technology wisely.

Professor Clifton F. Conrad penned chapter 4, "Change and Innovation in Graduate and Professional Education in Major Public Research Universities: The *Fin de Siècle* and Beyond." In it he sketches the UW–Madison's remarkable history of providing graduate education of the highest caliber, and the natural reluctance of faculty to that form. The chapter advances a template for graduate and professional education change and innovation through interdisciplinary programming, nondegree program alternatives, and varied program requirements including internships, compressed learning, the use of instructional technology, and enhancing community.

In chapter 5, "The Future of International Studies," Dean David M. Trubek looks at international studies in research universities during the twentieth century, as well as future challenges for the discipline. The chapter suggests a new vision of international studies by focusing on students' needs, which includes rethinking international education boundaries and creating new partnerships.

Historically, the state's businesses, industry, and agricultural and public sector groups all have had high expectations about the assistance the UW–Madison might provide. Chapter 6, "Public Access to University Expertise," by Professor Donald A. Nichols, reviews the public's historical and contemporary demand for advanced expertise from the UW–Madison, including the provision of advice to both advanced professionals and organizations. The chapter discusses the organizational challenges of public access to the UW–Madison's expertise, including campus and statewide political and social cultures, internal reward systems, and the widening gap between the nature of and the strength of the public and private higher education sectors. The chapter concludes by illustrating new examples and future opportunities for the UW–Madison in this area.

In chapter 7, "A Great Undergraduate University," Professor William Cronon provides a philosophical and historical underpinning of undergraduate education, and discusses why research universities need to be committed to providing the highest possible quality undergraduate education. The chapter suggests that the UW–Madison must couple the rigor and depth of the research enterprise with the breadth and depth that come from great undergraduate teaching.

I invite you to consider how the authors' visions, and the questions they pose, can be woven into our dialogue about the future of UW–Madison. I challenge you to help the university shape a better tomorrow just as our visionary Wisconsin pioneers did 150 years ago when they laid the foundation for a great state university. We owe them nothing less as the UW–Madison enters the next century.

I want to thank the contributing authors for volunteering their time and thoughts to this historic project. Their suggestions and discussions were crucial to the framing of this volume. I want to also acknowledge the University of Wisconsin Foundation for their support for this book. Finally, I thank Noel Radomski, who coordinated the many aspects of this project and saw the book through from start to finish.

David Ward
Chancellor

The Challenges of Irreversible Change in Higher Education

THE UNIVERSITY OF WISCONSIN–MADISON IN THE 1990s

David Ward

AMERICAN HIGHER EDUCATION is in the midst of a sea change, although it is one that is largely unrecognized. University-based research and programs document and analyze changes in the global economy and in the social policies of government on institutions and individuals. We seem, however, to be uneasy about confronting the irreversible effects of the same changes on higher education. This reluctance is understandable. Since World War II we have enjoyed an era of unprecedented expansion, success, and recognition, and in viewing the more ominous signs of the current decade, we are experiencing a natural and somewhat paralytic nostalgia about our past. Of course, prior to World War II, universities survived periods of rapid shifts in public support and coped with the extraordinary circumstances of the Great Depression and the war itself. Throughout its history, American higher education has responded to periodic changes in its external environment, and whether this is widely-acknowledged or not, I contend that public higher education, in general—and the University of Wisconsin–Madison, in particular—is currently adapting to changes in many of the underlying conditions that made its success possible in the decades following the end of World War II. The question now is whether or not we are also developing new, viable strategies for maintaining our preeminence

David Ward is Andrew H. Clark Professor of Geography and chancellor of the University of Wisconsin–Madison.

in the twenty-first century. Much that we currently cherish in our past is derived from the creative responses and strategic anticipations of our predecessors, and we are in a sense privileged to be actors in an era demanding similar attributes.

Public research universities were created through a fusion of at least three distinct nineteenth-century educational traditions: a commitment to general education derived from the venerable New England liberal arts college; a commitment to access and practicality rooted in the land grant tradition; and a commitment to basic research based upon the precedents of graduate education in German universities. These American hybrids were slowly nurtured during the first half of the twentieth century, then they brilliantly flowered after World War II. For about four decades after 1945, we experienced a "golden age" in American higher education. Public research universities expanded at a rapid pace, benefiting from massive infusions of federal and state dollars. Initially ignited by grants provided by the GI Bill, student enrollments expanded rapidly, and later federal funding of research accelerated and sustained an unprecedented expansion of knowledge. Certainly, the University of Wisconsin (and after merger legislation of 1971, the University of Wisconsin–Madison) built its national and international reputation on access, affordability, and the quality of its teaching, research, and outreach.

The vastly expanded scale of public research universities did, however, challenge their capacity to provide an appropriate balance between the various components of their mission as they tried to become many things to many people. At the same time, this was an era of both intense disciplinary specialization of academic programs and research and a growing functional specialization in administrative and student services. Despite the sustained growth and intense creativity associated with this period, public research universities began to look and behave much more like large, complex bureaucracies than the traditional collegial structures so long associated with university life. Professional academic staff provided most of the key administrative and service functions, and faculty became anchored in disciplinary departments that were often better connected with similar departments in peer institutions worldwide than with related departments in their own university. There were growing anxieties about a loss of any sense of a university-based academic community.

To illustrate these shifts in the scale and organization of research universities, one only has to look at the role of the president or chancellor. Fifty years ago, the typical leader of a public research university had a deep personal knowledge of the various parts of the organization. The administration and much of the institution was staffed by generalists who had an intuitive sense of the needs of faculty, staff, and students. Today's academic leader is managing a much more diverse and complex enterprise, with far less personal knowledge of its individual parts and functions and with a far greater commitment to public relations and external constituencies. In short, during this "golden age" of growth and specialization there was a massive refabrication of public research universities and, sadly, a loss of internal coherence. During the 1960s, much of this apprehension was expressed through critiques from within universities themselves, but eventually the more compelling and divisive debates about the war in Vietnam obscured and perhaps buried concerns about our institutional culture.

The revival of these institutional concerns began as isolated expressions of cynicism in the mid-1980s, but by the early 1990s, public suspicions about educational quality and institutional values had grown into a torrent of criticism. Suddenly, and with some justification, the images of our vaunted institutions of higher learning had become tarnished. Typically, in these critiques, we were the victims of assassination by anecdote. But there was a core of truth to many of the indictments. Students, parents, policymakers, and commentators openly questioned whether public research universities featured the proper balance of teaching, research, and outreach. Had we forsaken the basic mission of undergraduate education? Were many of our faculty inaccessible to students? Was their research arcane and inaccessible as well? Was there still utility in our outreach efforts? Did we care whether or not our teaching assistants could communicate effectively? Why did graduate students take six, seven, even eight or more years to earn the Ph.D.? And why did a Ph.D. fail to yield appropriate employment? These questions contributed to an atmosphere in which strong responses were needed.

Responses to Public Anxieties

Every aspect of our mission was fodder for spirited debate. As public concern swelled, the leadership and key faculty and staff of public research universities began to understand and acknowledge existing imbalances; in my judgment, our responsiveness has been underestimated. Appropriately, enhancing undergraduate education was at the heart of most of our responses, and the UW–Madison was at the forefront of these efforts. A faculty- and staff-driven blueprint entitled "Future Directions: The University in the 21st Century" was the cornerstone of our response. This remarkable self-evaluation, performed in conjunction with the reaccreditation process in 1988, provided our agenda for addressing many public anxieties. The report was a candid recognition of the limitations of public research universities and offered six major recommendations:

- Recruit, develop, and retain the best faculty, staff, and students.
- Strengthen undergraduate education.
- Excel in research.
- Strengthen the university's commitment to public service.
- Ensure an environment of equity and diversity.
- Integrate academic planning and budgeting.

On the basis of subsequent discussions three additional directions were added:
- Improve assessment and accountability.

- Support a greater awareness of campus community.
- Strengthen external relations.

The report also argued that success in the implementation of these directions would be dependent upon an ability to address several concerns about the current state of the university. These concerns were expressed as a set of assumptions about changes that would be necessary for the university to successfully implement its directions. These changes included the need for a broader understanding of the university's educational mission; an enhanced sense of the university as a community fostering the development of new knowledge and responding to changing technological needs; an improved resource allocation among competing needs; a clearer setting of goals and priorities by the colleges and schools within the university; and a better management of enrollments to fit the university's strengths.

"Future Directions" was a call to change; it carried the legitimacy of a self-study involving the full range of university constituencies. We turned our considerable research capabilities inward. We developed student surveys, sought feedback from focus groups, and enlisted the involvement of faculty and staff governance. We confirmed many of the problems associated with undergraduate education and recognized the absence of any overall plan to assist freshmen in their transition from high school to college. Spotty undergraduate advising, particularly in the first two years, was a huge barrier to achievement. Some students were frustrated by difficulties in class access, making it easier to justify registering for courses based on convenient time slots rather than academic coherence. The adoption of computerized registration with a longer lead time provided the needed flexibility to open and reschedule required and popular courses. The improvement and expansion of a summer orientation program for new students and their parents included enhanced advising. The development of the Cross-College Advising Service has improved advising for students who have not declared their major. Nevertheless, there is still much room for improvement in undergraduate advising. The demands on advisers continue to grow in relation to students' anxieties about future employment, about time-to-degree, and about access to required courses that serve as gateways to degree programs.

Other responses to concerns about the quality of undergraduate education were more directly concerned with the curriculum and the learning experience. The quantitative and communications components of the general education requirement were enhanced and provided additional incentives for freshmen and sophomores to take small classes. Efforts to increase the involvement of undergraduates in research and in the use of instructional technology were especially creative. Using private funds from the Hilldale Trust, we created undergraduate research fellowships—opportunities for students to pair with faculty and engage in original research during the summer between their junior and senior years. More recently a somewhat different program has been developed to address the needs of first- and second-year students. Several of our residence halls were designated as learning communities by linking them to specific curricular themes. The Bradley Learning Community, in particular, attracted interest as a contemporary expression of the experimental college ideals of Alexander Meiklejohn, which briefly flourished before World War II. And using a combination of public and private funds (including a special tuition supplement supported by students), we vastly improved student access to computers and email and thereby made faculty and staff more accessible. Faculty and staff brought a new commitment to undergraduate education, and their role was crucial in enhancing the recognition of teaching and undergraduate learning. The increased number and heightened visibility of teaching awards was demonstrated by recognition both at the campuswide level and within individual schools and colleges. A more explicit justification of teaching quality was required in the preparation of tenure cases.

Many academic leaders here and elsewhere were puzzled by

the low level of public appreciation for our energetic responses. Eventually, we realized that our activities were largely unrecognized because the results we had achieved were those that students and their parents believed we should have reached anyway. These responses were intended to, and did, re-energize our commitment to undergraduate education but largely within the existing paradigms of public higher education. But while we were struggling to adapt and respond to this era of sobering fault-finding, the ground was shifting beneath us. And these shifts were not mere tremors, but realignments of seismic proportion.

A convergence of trends—fiscal, demographic, technical, and intellectual—has produced changes in many of the underlying assumptions of higher education for the past forty years. No single one of these trends alone could radically alter the environment of higher education, but together they have created a new set of strategic challenges.

The most clearly recognizable of these trends is the dramatic shift in the composition of our funding. Our revenues are derived from four distinct sources. First, state appropriations and, to a much lesser degree, tuition have historically supplied the basic and largest proportion of our budget. Second, federal funds, obtained competitively by faculty and staff, largely fueled the research engine and, in addition, provided much of the support for graduate students. Third, a set of endowments sustained by private gifts and intellectual properties has for many years provided the competitive margin of excellence. The balance comes from the auxiliary revenues of services provided to students, the campus, and the community. But the political economy of higher education has changed substantially in the last two decades, resulting in shifts in every aspect of our funding mix.

Shifts in State and Federal Funding

In Wisconsin the state's proportionate commitment to the UW–Madison has dropped from about one-half to about one-quarter of our total revenues. Historically, the state was the dominant player in our budget, and legislators attempted to balance appropriations in order to set tuition as low as possible. For most of this century, the combination of tax dollars and tuition always exceeded 60 percent of our budget, but today, these two sources provide only 40 percent of our revenues. Of course for most of this period the absolute amount of state support continued to increase; it is only during the present decade that program appropriations have actually declined. The impacts of these revenue shifts have also been uneven within the university. In the health sciences, for example, the increased dependence on clinical revenues and on patient reimbursements necessitated the creation of a public authority to manage the University Hospital and the reorganization of the clinical activities of the faculty as the UW Medical Foundation. As entrepreneurial revenues exceeded those derived from state appropriations, the need for greater flexibility and autonomy in the management of the university became a topic of debate. With virtually no state support, the University Hospital represents an alternative management model of a public enterprise that has been enjoyed more broadly by universities in other states.

UW–Madison was not alone in confronting these fiscal changes; most other public universities faced similar reductions in state support. Like other states, Wisconsin shifted social spending priorities toward building prisons and reducing property taxes. Unlike many other states with universities of similar quality, Wisconsin found itself limited by a relatively modest tax-paying population base and by a commitment to low tuition. Elsewhere more aggressive tuition policies helped to cushion the effects of fiscal policies but exacerbated public anxieties regarding the affordability of a college education. Federal financial aid, increasingly in the form of loans, now dominates the public support of tuition, while living costs and the growth of student debt (which represents a serious future liability) is now a key issue in the debate about college costs.

Despite relatively low tuition and modest levels of student debt, UW–Madison has not escaped the national media frenzy over the cost of a college education, a frenzy provoked primarily by the annual tuition levels of $20,000 at most elite private universities. State policymakers, nationwide, have increasingly moved the costs of public higher education from state tax appropriations to tuition. They are willing to raise tuition to compensate for the loss of state support. That is not the case in Wisconsin, where we are faced with two possible approaches. Either we maintain our traditionally low tuition levels at the expense of quality or we implement a variable tuition model in which larger amounts of financial aid are available to offset the higher tuition costs for lower-income families.

In contrast, federal research support was an extremely stable part of the university's budget, and for the past quarter-century it has provided over one-quarter of the university's budget. UW–Madison has consistently ranked among the top three public universities in research revenues from federal agencies. But when deficit reduction became the preoccupation of the 1990s, the main source for resources and for research and graduate education was put in serious jeopardy. Indeed, certain categories of that federal support, mainly in the arts and humanities, were sharply reduced, and still show no sign of rebounding despite the rosier federal budget outlook. Selected areas of the social, physical, and biological sciences have, however, held their own or even increased their appropriations. In response to the uncertainty of federal funding, faculty and staff have developed a variety of alternative industrial and foundation sources of research funding, which now account for about 9 percent of our revenues.

A Greater Role for Private Funding

Private and philanthropic sources have had more dramatic effects on the capital budget of the university. Cutting-edge research efforts required either state-of-the-art buildings or expensive remodeling of existing structures. Undergraduate teaching facilities required massive updating to make use of instructional technology and to reflect newer teaching methods and laboratory techniques. UW–Madison began to aggressively seek and use private gifts to support these urgently needed improvements. From 1970 to 1990, the State of Wisconsin provided about 90 percent of the costs of construction on the UW–Madison campus, but thereafter the proportions shifted dramatically. Grainger Hall of Business was the first major campus facility constructed with a very large private anchor gift, which, when combined with other gifts provided one-half of the total construction cost. Soon after, WISTAR (Wisconsin Initiative in Science, Technology and Research) made possible the planning and construction of several new science facilities, including Genetics, Biotechnology, Biochemistry, and Engineering Research centers with the proviso that 50 percent of the cost was to be raised by the university. A successor program, Healthstar, designed to promote the construction of new health science facilities, is based on an agreement that the university will raise two-thirds of the cost.

The new southeast campus marvel, the Kohl Center, was a $76 million project built with no state tax dollars. We must now shoulder considerable responsibility for attracting private funds to campus construction projects and, fortunately for UW–Madison, our loyal alumni and friends have displayed great altruism, allowing us to pursue many of our most urgently needed projects and programs. We are also realizing major gains in the quality and speed with which these buildings are completed and, over the last decade, we have experienced a campus building boom.

While most private contributions to the university were nurtured by the UW Foundation, which currently provides almost 10 percent of our operating budget, it is important to note that UW Madison was one of the first research universities, public or private, to recognize the potential economic value of the intellectual property of its faculty. Our assumption is that faculty and staff have an obligation to the institution that harbors and encourages their work. The Wisconsin Alumni Research Foundation (WARF) is one of the oldest entities of its kind. Created with the funds from a few very early patents, WARF is a highly successful endowment, based on its success in licensing the intellectual property of faculty and staff. Forced to be more competitive on all fronts, public research universities, including UW Madison, are forming and solidifying their public/private partnerships. University research parks are a relatively new outgrowth of research universities. Faculty and staff whose research interests spawn commercially-viable processes and products either license their intellectual property or leave the university to start up their own businesses. When possible, universities attempt to keep these businesses close to home in their research parks. The UW–Madison Research Park, located on the former farmlands of the College of Agricultural and Life Sciences, houses more than seventy businesses. Many other spin-offs are located in the local community.

The impact of private funding on the public research university also raises questions of integrity and identity. Clear procedures are needed to regulate the relationships between private parties and the university in order to avoid inappropriate influence and conflicts of interest. Private gifts also have the potential to alter the direction or mission of the university. At UW–Madison, as at many public research universities, we find that most of the private gifts have been directed to our professional schools. That trend could threaten the basic liberal arts mission of the university. Fortunately, over the past few years, our liberal arts programs have also benefited from the generosity of their alumni, albeit somewhat modestly.

Demographic Shifts

Along with the new fiscal realities, we are faced with new demographic realities. All universities have struggled to serve an increasingly diverse population. The stakes are high, because if we do not find effective ways to serve a wider variety of constituencies, we will lose our public legitimacy. To offer the finest possible educational experience we must have diverse faculty, staff, and student populations. For long we have prided ourselves on the contributions made by our diverse international student body to our educational environment. We must also value the educational impact of an inclusiveness that reaches the full range of identities within the United States. Furthermore, public universities are responsible for serving society most broadly. And many future employers of our students, such as major corporations, are demanding that we educate alumni of diverse backgrounds. At the same time, there is an intense national public debate about affirmative action programs, and a number of our peer universities are under legal attack for their admissions procedures. In California, for example, racial considerations in admissions have resulted in major reductions within public higher education in the numbers of students of color entering public research universities like UC–Berkeley and UCLA. In Texas, the Hopwood decision, issued by a federal appellate court, has sharply reduced the ability of that state's public universities to recruit students of color. The University of Michigan is currently defending a legal challenge to its admissions process.

In Wisconsin, where there has been modest progress in recruiting and retaining students of color, there has been a more muted public reaction to the affirmative action debate. We have examined our current diversity efforts, found them lacking, and are now struggling to fashion creative recruitment strategies that meet both the letter of the law and the spirit of our mission. Attempts to regulate admission to the different institutions of the UW System have further complicated our efforts. An enrollment management policy designed to limit student access in relation to state support, combined with the large tuition discrepancy between UW–Madison and its peer institutions in other states, has made admission much more competitive. For these reasons we have to be more effective in our collaborations with the K–12 educational system to help expand the pool of students from underrepresented groups who are qualified to attend our universities. We are committed to the enhancement of pre-service and continuing teacher training; to the expansion of precollege programs to K–12 students at various levels; to the support of scholarly research on K–12 issues; and to the development of direct partnerships with schools and communities to address local needs.

Educational needs are also evolving in response to changes in life cycles and career trajectories. More people now need to retrain or to update their skills during the course of their working lives; older and returning adult students comprise a rapidly increasing proportion of our student body. The demand for life-long learning opportunities with enhanced access to our courses and facilities has also engaged us very directly with the inexorable advance in digital communication.

Communications and Information Revolution

Universities and K–12 schools share the challenge of determining the degree to which the communications/information revolution drives the way we teach and what we teach our students. We know that some aspects of this revolution have been overstated; some of the pedagogical promises have not yet been fulfilled. However, we must fully face our obligation to discern which aspects of this revolution will ultimately benefit our students and make our institutions more accessible and effective. At UW–Madison these changes provoked the creation of the Division of Information Technology (DoIT), which combined several smaller units into a new cross-cutting campuswide organization and has subsequently restructured the development and delivery of improved facilities and services.

Communications and information gathering, analysis, and retrieval processes are improving at a rapid pace. At the heart of this revolution is, of course, the computer. Advances in computer chip development and memory storage are occurring at awesome speeds. The powerful and immensely popular information super-highway is already inadequate for meeting the needs of the academic research community, and its successor, Internet 2, is being developed. All of the hardware and software innovations and the dramatic improvements in communications methods have potential educational implications. To what degree will or should they drive changes in what is taught, or how it is taught? Information technology already has transformed the way our libraries operate. We can access information from our desktops, and we can search collections locally and across the country. To date, however, although instructional technology has produced profound changes in some courses, few academic departments or programs have systematically transformed themselves through the use of new technologies. Indeed, most recognized research universities are extremely tentative in their strategic responses to the rapid growth of distance education as start-up ventures.

Historically universities have developed curricula and teaching methods strictly based on what faculty members believed students should know and how they believed that knowledge should be delivered. However, changes in public expectations, the impact of instructional technology, competition from nonuniversity-based learning, and the explosion of new knowledge all, to one degree or another, exert some influence over this process. We need to be more cognizant of the differing needs of our students and to offer courses and learning opportunities that respond to those needs. For example, universities have tended to teach some courses such as math and languages as though all students were pursuing degrees in those subjects. Yet, proficiency rather than mastery may be a student's goal in a particular area. By developing multiple learning contexts, we can meet the needs of the students who are just seeking a threshold or basic knowledge in a subject. But large-scale systemic instructional change demands massive investments in technology and training, and the argument that information technology can save money is probably exaggerated and certainly premature.

Shifts in the Intellectual Division of Labor

Collaboration with scholars across the ocean is something most of our faculty and staff members take for granted. Again, thanks largely to the power of the computer and advanced communications technologies, there are few barriers to working with colleagues anywhere on the globe. Yet there are significant organizational barriers to collaborating with campus colleagues across departmental or programmatic boundaries. When such collaboration succeeds, it is largely due to individual resourcefulness rather than institutional intent. For generations, faculty members have been rewarded for increasingly specialized research within disciplinary or even subdisciplinary mineshafts. During that same period, the disciplinary departments became the dominant element in the organization of universities. This organizational model supported the rapid development of new knowledge and has served us, and society, extremely well. Of course, the intellectual division of labor was always connected by a variety of interdisciplinary programs, but, ironically, many of these programs developed a professional identity indistinguishable from that of departments. Most faculty members were rightly convinced that this departmental status was the key to resources and prestige.

Nevertheless, there is a growing awareness of the limitations of our organizational and professional cultures. How should we better support the expansion of knowledge that is arising from more than one discipline? Are there improved structures, or are there better incentives that would encourage the cross-fertilization of ideas? But the architecture of knowledge itself is changing and while the deconstruction of some disciplines has created an almost individual level of specialization, others have creatively combined their foci into larger arenas of inquiry. While we often complain of the impacts of fiscal, demographic and technical shifts on the traditional roles of scholars, changes in the intellectual division of labor may actually alter the research university more profoundly than any exogenous factor.

In summary, the new fiscal realities, the demographic shifts, the information revolution, and the issues surrounding the intellectual division of labor—each of these elements may have varying degrees of influence, but, when taken together, they are causing a significant, and, I would maintain, irreversible change in public research universities. Since shifts in public policy and popular opinion are often cyclical, it is tempting take solace in the expectation that if we wait long enough, the pendulum will swing back to a more familiar and comfortable position. Our successful efforts to rebalance our mission may be inadequate unless we also confront the degree to which several irreversible changes will determine our future.

From Directions to Connections

These changes do, however, have one common impact. They all involve shifts in the ways in which the university is connected both internally and externally. Changes in the composition of our revenues push us to be more connected and accountable to our traditional sources and, at the same time, to reach out to establish new connections and partnerships. Demographic shifts demand improved connections with the growing diversity of American society, with our K–12 school systems, and with continuous learners of every age. The communication/information age is driving exponential changes in our capacity to make worldwide connections and to collaborate at any distance. And the trends toward the deconstruction and reconstruction of disciplines also creates new connections. How we respond to these challenges and how we seize the opportunities to direct them will profoundly affect our ability to exert intellectual leadership in the next century.

Our efforts to confront these challenges were proposed in the spring of 1995, when we issued a document entitled "A Vision for the Future: Priorities for UW–Madison for the Next Decade." The vision put forth in that document centers on a central theme of "learning" and a commitment not only to enhance our mission by doing things differently but also by doing different things. Rather than continuing our efforts to rebalance teaching, research, and service as if they were distinct and separate activities, we organized our priorities around three interconnected systems of learning: **the learning experience, the learning community, and the learning environment.**

We aspire to expand the **learning experience** well beyond the traditional classroom to include residential learning communities, voluntary service opportunities, enhanced uses of informational technology, increased field and research opportunities, and by viewing education as an opportunity to advance learning. The promotion of **learning communities** involves the support of improved connections and collaborations across traditional disciplinary boundaries and expanded partnerships with a wide range of external constituencies. The **learning environment** conducive to these learning experiences and communities requires the wider application of information technology to improve instruction, administrative services, and external communications. An integrated and comprehensive campus master plan was also developed to facilitate the development of a new learning environment. Among the proposals within the plan were building designs that would combine the needs of several disciplines while also serving the needs of external constituents.

To advance toward this vision, the document outlined four priorities supported by five key systems. These priorities are:

- Maintaining our research preeminence.
- Reconceptualizing undergraduate education.
- Joining the global community.
- Updating the Wisconsin Idea.

The five supporting systems are:

- Maximizing our human resources.
- Re-thinking our organization.
- Encouraging collaboration.

- Using technology wisely.
- Renewing the campus physical environment.

These priorities and systems have served as a systemic framework for a range of voluntary initiatives over the past three years. Many cross-campus initiatives have been undertaken, with discretionary funds supporting these priorities. Schools, colleges, departments, and administrative divisions have developed initiatives to advance the campus vision. Now, three years later, through the collective efforts of hundreds of faculty, staff, and students across campus, we can identify many striking achievements and many more projects in progress. The related priorities of the campus vision created a stronger sense of the need for institutional alignment, and the framework encouraged the participants in individual initiatives to build toward some larger common achievement. Most of the initiatives proposed by the "Future Directions" report improved on long-established practices, and more innovative developments were at the level of pilot projects. We can celebrate the success of our innovative pilots, but our vision priorities pushed us to the next level.

If the Bradley experiment is providing a more effective learning environment for students, how can we offer opportunities like this to any student who is interested? Does the restructuring of the biological sciences stand as a precedent for other divisions? If some disciplines have succeeded in interdisciplinary teaching and/or research enterprises, what can be learned from them that can help support the success of others? How can we learn when and where interdisciplinary enterprises promise success? If the Division of Information Technology (DoIT) can combine separate units into a cross campus organization, how many other distinct services ought to consider a merger movement?

There are, in fact, several examples of a larger and more ambitious scale of innovation. The opening of the Chadbourne Residential College created a new scale in opportunities for students to participate in programs based in residence halls; it has

University of Wisconsin - Madison
Mission, Vision, Priorities

Mission:
To create, integrate, transfer and apply knowledge.

Vision Themes

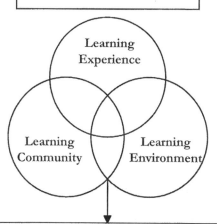

Priorities

Maintaining our research preeminence.	Reconceptualizing undergraduate education.	Joining the global community.	Updating the Wisconsin Idea.

Priority Systems

Maximizing our human resources.	Rethinking our organization.	Encouraging collaboration.	Using technology wisely.	Renewing the campus physical environment.

also facilitated improvements and changes in the honors program. Among other educational initiatives are Cross-College Advising; the International Institute and the World Affairs and the Global Economy (WAGE) program; the Teaching Academy; collaboration within and among the undergraduate curricula of the life sciences; improved programs in the development of instructional technology in teaching; and the adoption of enhanced general education requirements for quantitative and communication skills. In response to the changing circumstances of affirmative action policies, new strategies have been developed for the recruitment of undergraduates from schools with populations underrepresented at UW–Madison. These efforts place much more attention on early intervention in collaboration with the schools and future employers.

The adoption of a campus master plan also changed the scale and style of our response to the maintenance and improvement of our infrastructure. The Biotechnology Building had already set a new model for campus facilities by demonstrating how a facility could combine programs and serve a variety of constituencies. The much larger and more expensive Healthstar project includes an interdisciplinary clinical research center and a learning center shared by all three health science schools.

The master plan also considered the problems of how an expanding university could be a "good neighbor." This issue now forms part of the agenda of a University Relations team devoted to the strategic engagement of the university in its many private and public relationships.

We are also confronting the need to improve knowledge transfer and to ensure that the university retains appropriate intellectual property rights. WARF had provided a national model of this process for many years. The establishment of the Council on Technology Transfer is designed to build on that strength by improving the coordination of WARF, UIR (University-Industry Relations), URP (University Research Park), and the Graduate School as the primary sponsor of basic research. More challenging and more complex issues surround the coordination of the health sciences. The various components of the health science enterprise need realignment in order to provide incentives and support for research and teaching in an environment in which clinical and hospital revenues make major and essential contributions to the academic enterprise. Like other research universities, our library is also in the midst of similar challenges of revenues and mission. Research libraries have been devastated by increased serial costs at a time when major expenditures were necessary to improve access and circulation by means of information technology. The value of research publications is created by our faculty members, who grant their intellectual property to publishers and thereby contribute to the problem. Eventually, these economic circumstances, combined with the potentialities of digital communication, may create a means of redress. This possibility, however, will necessitate not only our own strategic response but also the decisive collaboration of all major research universities. The collaborative achievements of the libraries of the CIC (Committee on Institutional Cooperation) Universities, and the recent formation of UCAID (University Consortium for Advanced Internet Development) to create a second Internet that is more appropriate and responsive to educational needs, are precedents for future practices.

The absolute core of our mission is, however, the delivery of programs to our students that take advantage of the research capacities of our faculty. Two of our most recent initiatives are designed to change how we proceed in our most basic processes. A program to encourage collaborative faculty appointments in related programs attracted more than 90 proposals. The funding of five of these proposals for clustered appointments was enhanced by a state appropriation for similar sets of appointments in the life sciences. Almost all these proposals combined the faculty resources of several existing programs and reconstructed the intellectual division of labor by means of collaborative curricula rather than as new units. Among the proposals funded were

Biophotonics, Geonomics, Cognitive and Affective Neuroscience, and International Programs in Public Affairs. Another recent major initiative encourages the development of capstone degrees and certificates for students who have completed their under-graduate degree but require additional knowledge to connect them with a rapidly changing and increasingly technical employ-ment scene. These programs will, we hope, enlarge the standard conception of the master's degree and provide a range of self-paced residential and distance courses. This initiative also attract-ed additional support in the form of an award from the Sloan Foundation to extend the program to several specific life sciences. While the Ph.D. will retain its status and form within graduate education, master's degrees and related postgraduate certificates present many opportunities for us to be responsive to two chal-lenging issues: to address the changing needs of continuing edu-cation or life long learning and to encourage undergraduate stu-dents to focus more completely on the liberal arts and sciences before considering professional programs.

These accomplishments represent a historic level of alignment and commitment to connect different parts of the university; they involve faculty, staff, and students working across traditional boundaries and sharing a common vision. In many respects, a long tradition of shared governance, often viewed as an obstacle to change, actually facilitated and at times led the process. "Future Directions" was, after all, a broadly based self-study that includ-ed the various constituencies of the university. Subsequently, the academic planning councils of schools and colleges worked with deans and directors to adapt the priorities to the specific issues of different academic and service units. The executive committees of the faculty senate, academic staff assembly, and student govern-ment groups, along with the campus academic planning council, provided creative suggestions and developed initiatives of their own. But, then, UW–Madison has a tradition for breaking tradi-tions and charting the course for others to follow.

The Resources of Our Mission and Vision

In celebrating our sesquicentennial, we recognize and appreciate the proud history of the University of Wisconsin and the lasting commitment of the State of Wisconsin to our institution. At the same time, we are adjusting our mission to the irreversible changes of the past decade, and we will enter the next millennium as a somewhat different institution. We have also begun the process of the self-study required as a part of our NCA (North Central Association) accreditation process precisely one decade after the same process produced "Future Directions." We have an opportunity to evaluate our performance and to reconsider our priorities.

Our own discussions also provide an opportunity for spirited public debate: Can a state of this size and wealth continue to afford a preeminent, comprehensive research university with a global niche? Do the citizens of Wisconsin support us in our effort to maintain our place in the constellation of leading universities around the world? Are we going to have the same national and international presence in the twenty-first century as we have had in this century?

At a time of uncertain resources, of increased demands for access, of unclear pedagogical changes, and of shifting structures of research, it would be foolhardy for any one institution to attempt to respond completely and autonomously to these changes. Each institution within American higher education cannot be all things to all people. Yet too many institutions attempt to emulate the most expensive and challenging aspects of the comprehensive public research university. A more viable approach is the development of strategic niches. Each university or college would evaluate its strengths, explore its potential clientele, and pursue that niche to its fullest. This requires effective collaboration across institutions; but the benefits would be great, and would accrue to the individual institution and to higher education as a whole.

Currently UW–Madison is proud to be recognized as one of the very best institutions among a group of approximately thirty public universities that combine large undergraduate enrollments, graduate and professional schools, a broad ranging research agenda, and comprehensive public service. This status was unambiguously established at the turn of the nineteenth century, when UW–Madison was invited to be a founding member of the prestigious American Association of Universities. During the course of the next decade, the resources available to sustain thirty institutions of this stature will no longer be adequate. Some universities will become regionally rather than nationally prominent, and others will diminish the scope of their mission. The survivors will be those institutions with the means to ensure the margin of excellence that is recognized at a global level.

UW–Madison has always provided the margin of excellence and the resources for its competitive edge from its own endowment resources and from the success of its faculty in obtaining extramural funding. The key to our future is to find a way to guarantee a level of basic support from state appropriations and tuition that at least equals the average of our peer institutions. In the absence of this commitment, the leveraged federal and private support no longer provides that margin of excellence that defines the national and international stature of UW–Madison. These issues can only be resolved successfully if state policymakers, students, parents, alumni, and the citizens of Wisconsin accept the necessity of a threshold level of basic support.

Quite apart from these issues of revenue and quality, UW–Madison is independently facing the challenges of other equally challenging irreversible changes. The priorities and systems defined in the vision document were designed to address these changes. Our creative responses reveal an agility and flexibility positioning us to enact developments guaranteeing our influence on an uncertain future. The very least our predecessors would ask of us is that we remain as outstanding and effective in the twenty-first century as we have been in the twentieth.

The Future of the Liberal Arts

Phillip R. Certain

Introduction

This chapter on the future of the liberal arts provides not answers, but questions. It does not try to predict the future as much as it identifies issues whose resolution will help shape the future. Thus, its aims are inherently modest in scope. For those who want predictions, a list is provided in the appendix, accompanied by the admonition that such lists often provide more merriment to the future reader than enlightenment for the present.

This chapter both celebrates the significance of the liberal arts throughout history (and throughout the history of this university) and explores some of the challenges that face them today. The challenges discussed in the chapter—learning to focus in order to compete, preserving the scholarly community, understanding the nature of truth, protecting academic freedom, and accepting the imperative of relevance—will help determine the future of the liberal arts within a great public research university. If the challenges are met well, then the future of the liberal arts is bright indeed.

Phillip R. Certain is professor of chemistry and dean of the College of Letters and Science at the University of Wisconsin–Madison.

The Foundational Role of Liberal Arts within a Great Research University

"What is the answer?"

[I was silent]

"In that case, what is the question?"

—Gertrude Stein, last words from *Alice B. Toklas, What Is Remembered*

The "liberal arts" is a term that at once names the oldest subjects of human learning and describes the foundation of higher education in the United States. Roman scholars identified seven artes liberales that originated with the Egyptians and Greeks: three language arts—grammar, rhetoric, logic; and four mathematical arts—arithmetic, geometry, music, astronomy. These were the subjects (arts) for the education of citizens who had the freedom (liberty) to study. These seven subjects are the antecedents of the present-day multitude of subjects in the humanities, arts, and sciences.

In the modern research university, the liberal arts are foundational. Over the 150 years since the founding of the University of Wisconsin, the liberal arts have provided the core of instruction and research. The College of Letters and Science (L&S) is the liberal arts college of UW–Madison. It traditionally teaches 95 percent of all freshman-sophomore credits and awards about 55 percent of all undergraduate degrees. At the graduate level, L&S has produced about 45 percent of the masters and almost 50 percent of the doctorate degrees awarded at UW–Madison.

It is impossible to develop excellence in the professional schools without excellence in the liberal arts. Business depends on excellence in economics, ethics, mathematics, science, and foreign language. Law requires excellence in political science, history, sociology, and public policy. Engineering, agriculture, and the health sciences require excellence in science and mathematics. All require excellence in disciplines devoted to written and oral communication.

Nevertheless, the term "liberal arts" is often misunderstood, even within higher education. For example, many believe that the liberal arts refer to the humanities and arts alone, and exclude the social and natural sciences.

Another misconception about the liberal arts, particularly in today's occupation-oriented society, is that the liberal arts denote a particular lack of focus on and relevance to the world of work. Throughout their long history, the liberal arts in fact have been intensely practical. For the Greeks, they provided training to allow free people to become citizens. In the middle ages, they provided the basis for the priesthood. In the nineteenth century, the liberal arts provided the general education required for the law, medicine, and the ministry. Today, the liberal arts are still closely related to general education leading to the professions, and yet they are more than that. Liberal arts graduates are found in leadership positions in nearly every major occupation, including government, education, business, and industry.

It has never been easy to characterize the liberal arts fully, because they have had many manifestations over their long history. Today, the term "liberal arts college" conjures up a picture of a small, private school, with a tree-shaded campus, ivy-covered buildings, and intense student-professor interactions. This is certainly an honored part of the picture. Another manifestation is the elite private Ivy League university, such as Harvard, Princeton, or Yale. And yet a minority of liberal arts students is educated at such institutions. A larger group is educated instead at public institutions, many in liberal arts units embedded within the nation's largest and most distinguished public research universities.

Enrollments in 1996 in two- and four-year colleges and universities totaled some 14 million students, of whom 78 percent were enrolled in public institutions. Of the 3,700 institutions, only 88 are designated as Research I universities by the Carnegie Foundation, based on the size and scope of their programs.

Seventy percent of Research I universities are public. In addition to their major graduate education and research missions, these universities are among the largest undergraduate institutions. The University of Wisconsin–Madison has long held an honored place in this group.

Among the 90 largest institutions of higher education in the fall of 1995, with enrollments ranging from 22,350 to 70,000 students, there were 42 Research I publics, with a total enrollment of 1.2 million, and 6 Research I privates, with a total enrollment of 170 thousand. In contrast, the 166 selective liberal arts colleges denoted as Baccalaureate I colleges by the Carnegie Foundation have total enrollments of approximately 280 thousand students. While these numbers reflect total undergraduate enrollments, it is not atypical for liberal arts majors to comprise more than half of the graduates from major research universities. Thus, the health of the liberal arts in these institutions is of vital importance.

The preservation of the spirit of the liberal arts in higher education is uniquely American. What do these varieties of liberal arts college have in common? Certainly not size, nor student and faculty profiles, nor approaches to general education, nor administrative structure. But liberal arts colleges do share the following four common goals, and these will be important guides for the decisions that will ensure the centrality of the liberal arts in the future.

Education of the complete person. A hallmark of a liberal arts education is breadth of study spanning the humanities, arts, social sciences, biological sciences, and physical sciences. A concomitant goal is an integrated understanding that allows the educated person to be able to receive new information and experiences and place them in an understandable context. The ability to distinguish fact from fiction and the significant from the insignificant is an essential trait of the liberal arts graduate. A liberal education must therefore teach and encourage critical thinking and cogent communication.

Education for citizenship. The Jeffersonian ideal of a liberal education is that it enables the citizens to choose from among themselves the leaders who would best serve the democracy. This is also the essence of the Wisconsin Idea: education in service to the state. In addition, the liberal arts education must prepare students to understand with sophistication both a technological world and a world with rapidly changing economic as well as national boundaries. Graduating college students face a chaotic world that has lost its grounding in a shared sense of social and political order and values. A liberal arts education must help its graduates develop the skills, values, and attitudes to play influential roles in this world.

Education for a productive life. One important aspect of a productive life is a person's choice of jobs and careers, and a liberal arts education should attend to these practical aspirations of students. At the same time, a productive life is not always one that is constrained to a single path; many workers will change jobs and even careers several times during their lifetime. A liberal arts education must prepare students for their third job as well as for their first. A broad liberal arts education also prepares the graduate for a meaningful life outside of a formal work setting, a life that includes activities ranging from the arts to volunteer community service to living within a diverse community.

Education for lifelong learning. This aspect of a liberal education is dearest to the hearts of the faculty and to many students and graduates: the joy of learning to satisfy human curiosity even if the practical consequences cannot be predicted; the ecstasy of discovering for oneself truth and beauty. In today's practical, bottom-line oriented world, this often appears to be a luxury that universities can dispense with. But this short-sighted view ignores history: many of the ideas and devices that shape the practical world had their origins in a love of learning for its own sake. Can we afford to rob future generations of a legacy that our generation is so dependent upon? Education for the love of learning itself is the cornerstone of the liberal arts.

In addition to these commonly-held goals of the liberal arts, the College of Letters and Science at the University of Wisconsin–Madison is part of the land-grant tradition. This means that it is committed to providing access to higher education as broadly as possible, and it is committed to engagement with the larger society as part of the Wisconsin Idea.

The history of higher education in the U.S. is one of greater and greater access to higher education, but as the nation becomes more fractured, the story is far from over. For example, students whose parents earn incomes within the bottom quartile have less than a 10 percent chance of graduating from college. The probability for the top quartile is 80 percent. These facts have enormous implications for American democracy. The liberal arts are the central gateway for students into college, whether they obtain liberal arts or professional degrees. Thus the liberal arts, with the goal of education for citizenship, bear a critical responsibility for student access and success.

There have been at least five great expansions of access over the past 150 years, three of them realized and two still in process. The first came as the result of the Morrill Land Grant Act of 1862, which provided federal support for higher education in exchange for the development of the practical arts of engineering, agriculture, and military science. This act opened up higher education to thousands of farm youth who previously did not have access to it. Today, the land-grant universities provide the major intellectual capital for the nation.

Next, higher education was opened to women, although this is still not uniformly realized. While women are represented equitably in the undergraduate student body, they are still underrepresented in many majors at both the undergraduate and graduate level, and on the faculty.

After World War II, the G.I. Bill provided access to thousands of veterans who otherwise would never have had the opportunity for college. Their grandchildren now constitute the undergraduate student body.

Access to graduate education was transformed by the massive federal investment in science research in support of the race to the moon and in social science research in support of the Great Society programs. Research universities are primarily educational institutions and not primarily research institutes. Doing research is the most effective way to teach graduate students, and the results of research—both in discoveries and in educated students—enrich the nation. Graduate education and research also enrich the undergraduate liberal arts experience at the research university. Discoveries rapidly find their way into the curriculum, and undergraduates have rich opportunities to become directly involved in analyzing these discoveries. This is where the excitement of education for lifelong learning begins.

Finally, affirmative action programs growing out of the civil rights movement provided access to higher education for those ethnic groups that previously were largely absent from the nation's campuses. Progress has been slow even with federal initiatives, and much uncertainty lies ahead as affirmative action confronts contentious assertions about fairness and effectiveness. But history is on the side of increasing access, even if current affirmative action methods are swept away. History has taught that opening higher education to all citizens is not only desirable on idealistic grounds, it is essential to the preservation of the American democracy.

A commitment to access means a continuing commitment to a diverse faculty, staff, and student body. This is both an access and a fairness issue, but it is also more complicated than that. The liberal arts college is still too white and, in many disciplines, too male. Many liberal arts colleges reflect the hometowns of their students and not the world into which liberal arts graduates will enter and play a productive role. Thus, the liberal arts college cannot attain its goals of education for citizenship and for a productive life without an academic community that reflects the larger society.

The Wisconsin Idea—that the boundaries of the university are the boundaries of the state—is the Wisconsin articulation of the idea that universities exist to "do useful work." The joy of discovery and creation is undeniable, and one of the most precious attributes of the human spirit is doing useful work for posterity. Discoveries and creations unshared will not sustain the liberal arts. Not all individuals within the liberal arts are expected to provide direct useful work to the general public, but those who do should be given special appreciation. And within the university, all liberal arts faculty members have useful work to do with respect to their students and their colleagues.

Useful work increasingly involves interdisciplinary work. The problems both of society and of the intellect do not always conform easily to the current disciplinary boundaries. Take for example the "simple" question of restoration of prairie land within a semiurban setting. The ecologist is needed, to be sure. But the urban planner, the political scientist, the economist, and the civil engineer should also be at the table. Or, consider the development of understanding to guide U.S. foreign policy. Here, historians, sociologists, political scientists, anthropologists, geographers, as well as experts in literature, language, and art might be called upon. It is worthwhile to debate whether students should be educated strictly within disciplinary boundaries, or within interdisciplinary programs, but the support of interdisciplinary endeavors is a corollary to the liberal arts goal of education of the complete person.

As long the goals of the liberal arts and the land-grant tradition are valued, the liberal arts will keep their place in the center of U.S. higher education. But liberal arts colleges will face challenges in the future, five of which will be discussed here. This is not an exhaustive list, but it does focus on issues that are generating considerable discussion today. The approach here is to explicate general principles and philosophies, rather than to provide specific answers and strategies. It would be extraordinarily interesting to be able to look back fifty years from now to see how effective this approach had turned out to be.

The Challenge of Competition

> The university bureaucracy really works as an anti-bureaucracy, whose ideal is to allow the greatest number of individuals to pursue their own private interests with the least possible interaction.
> —David Damrosch, *We Scholars*

> I shall take it as understood that the faculty own the university, and that competition among universities is a competition among faculties.
> —Stephen M. Stigler, *The Research University in a Time of Discontent*

The future of the liberal arts in major research universities is completely intertwined with the future of the university as a whole. For public universities the next ten years are bound to be extraordinarily competitive for state support, for extramural funds, and for outstanding faculty and graduate students. (Competition for undergraduates is usually not a major issue for public research universities.) Many believe that at the end of this ten-year period, there will be fewer truly national public research universities than there are now. All top-tier universities are formulating plans to stay in that elite group, and their liberal arts units are key to their success. Nevertheless, liberal arts colleges also face internal competition for resources to maintain faculty, facilities, and programs.

Competition for state support is largely a local issue, turning on state-specific political environments, but the results have national and international significance. The three states that have been the most successful in sustained achievement in higher education have been California, Michigan, and Wisconsin. The populations of these three states and their per capita personal incomes in 1997 were, respectively, 32.3 million, $26,570; 9.8 million, $25,560; and 5.2 million, $24,475. In 1997–98, on a per-student basis these three states spent virtually the same amount: $3,926; $3,982; and $4,087 respectively. Thus, measured against personal income levels, Wisconsin citizens are the most generous.

For the past one hundred years, Wisconsin has kept pace with its larger competitors because of this generosity. Over just the past two years, however, the percentage increase in state support for higher education has been 24 percent in California, 11 percent in Michigan, and only 3 percent in Wisconsin. In inflation-adjusted dollars, tax support of higher education in Wisconsin has dropped 8 percent in ten years.

A major public policy decision faces Wisconsin, a decision that will determine the future of its flagship research university, and the liberal arts have a central role to play. The foundation of any public research university is undergraduate education, and liberal arts departments and programs play a major role in undergraduate teaching and student advising. If they play this role well, they encourage the state support that allows the institution to maintain its reputation in research.

Competition for extramural support has both a local and a national component. The local component is the support given through gifts from alumni and friends of the university. All public universities are becoming more "private-like" in terms of the degree to which they rely on gifts to stay competitive. The liberal arts are beneficiaries of this trend, but it is generally much harder for a liberal arts college in a public research university to attract major gifts, compared to the professional schools. There are several reasons for this. Often donors feel that the liberal arts core of the university is the public's responsibility, particularly in terms of buildings. Also, liberal arts graduates who acquire great wealth do so in areas seemingly unrelated to their liberal arts experience. But there are two more significant reasons why it is difficult to attract donor support. First, liberal arts colleges in major research universities are large and do not spend sufficient attention planting seeds of loyalty within their undergraduates and then nurturing those relationships. Second, because of the breadth of their programs, liberal arts colleges have a difficult time focusing their message and identifying potential donors. Particularly for the humanities and arts, it is critical that liberal arts colleges develop a stronger base of support among alumni donors.

The national component of competition for extramural support is in the arena of federal and foundation support. Wildly varying predictions about the future of federal support of research appear from equally reputable sources, but all would agree that the future will be more competitive, not less. The liberal arts college of a major research university is not only the undergraduate teaching engine of the university, it is also a major research engine. Thus, competition to remain among the best means staying competitive in research and scholarship in the liberal arts.

Competition for high-quality faculty is a precondition for successful competition for state support and extramural funds. Major research universities have always been competitive with one another for faculty, both for beginning faculty and senior scholars.

Different sorts of universities have had different philosophies. For the "elite Eastern schools," such as Harvard and Yale, the philosophy has been to tenure only those faculty who have achieved extraordinary distinction *elsewhere*. These institutions appoint younger scholars, most of whom have no chance to gain tenure, to carry out much of the teaching function of the university, even while they are also establishing themselves in research so that they can get a good job at another university after six or seven years.

The philosophy has been different at the major public research universities. Here the strategy has been to recruit the best young faculty possible, give them as many resources as possible to become successful, and try to build loyalty so that "raids" from other universities will prove inadequate. The expectation has been that everyone hired as an assistant professor will be promoted to tenure, not because tenure is easy, but because the institution chooses carefully at the beginning.

Neither of these strategies is pure, and in recent years both have become strained. The strategy of always hiring senior faculty from another institution has become particularly difficult in the sciences because of the phenomenal costs of establishing or moving a major research laboratory. At the same time, younger scientists are reluctant to set up a laboratory, only to have to move it in a few years. While the growth of endowments has allowed these institutions to go "boutique shopping" for faculty, one wonders what will happen in more austere economic times.

For public universities, there have always been opportunities for top scholars to move from one institution to another to improve their intellectual environment or personal rewards. In recent years, however, this phenomenon has seemed to become more democratized, as faculty who are not truly at the top of their profession receive offers that are not truly from peer (or better) universities. This phenomenon is very damaging to a liberal arts college, because it fosters the not unreasonable assumption that the best way to achieve a significant boost in salary is to get an outside offer—*any* outside offer. The successful liberal arts colleges of the future will find a way to get this problem under control, possibly by looking upon faculty retentions as strategically as faculty recruitments.

Turning now to the issue of internal competition for resources, it is fairly easy to make the abstract case for the centrality of the liberal arts, and to argue that the excellence of the university depends on excellence in the liberal arts. Translating that conviction into resources is difficult. Just as with external fund raising, the two major obstacles are size and focus.

All university budgets go through good times and bad times, and liberal arts colleges in research universities are often hurt during both swings of the pendulum. The math is simple. The liberal arts college or colleges represent the major portion of the university's budget. Thus, when there is a budget cut it is difficult to give the liberal arts units anything other than their percentage share. To do less would decimate the smaller units. Then when times get better, the university can fully restore the budgets of smaller units with funds that apparently would do little for the major liberal arts units. (This of course ignores the fact that liberal arts colleges are made up of individual departments, some of which are larger than the smaller schools and colleges of the university.) This is why, typically, the liberal arts colleges at major universities are chronically underfunded. The underfunding has accumulated over decades, and decades will be required to correct the pattern.

The second internal obstacle in the competition for resources is the demand for focus. This is an extraordinarily important issue because new resources are likely to become available only for specific purposes. If the liberal arts college does not identify attractive foci, it will not get new resources. If it identifies trendy foci that do not have potential for continued development, it will recruit faculty whose work will become rapidly irrelevant. The stakes are high.

The requirement for focus is a major break from the past. Previously, the liberal arts college decided on what departments and programs it most wanted to support and then attempted to hire the best faculty to staff these units. The faculty had the major responsibility for both the teaching and research activities of the unit. Now, those who are providing the funds are much more likely to say: "tell me what I am buying before you get the money." "Ensuring an excellent philosophy department" must compete with "Solving the human genome problem." Liberal arts colleges must learn how to compete in this environment without destroying themselves in the process.

Liberal arts colleges are used to competition. The challenge is to recognize the new rules of competition and then compete to ensure excellence in the future.

The Challenge of Community

> Imagine, my dear friend, if you can, a society formed of
> all the nations of the world . . . people having different
> languages, beliefs, opinions: in a word, a society without
> roots, without memories, without prejudices, without
> routines, without common ideas, without a national
> character, yet a hundred times happier than our own. . . .
> What serves as the link among such diverse elements?
> What makes all of this into one people?
>
> —Alexis de Tocqueville, 1831

In the years since de Tocqueville wrote those words, America has
formed roots, memories, prejudices, routines, and common ideas.
And yet de Tocqueville's two questions are timeless. Surely, higher education has played an important role in shaping the
American character, and a challenge for the liberal arts is to continually forge those links that de Tocqueville sought.

The concept of community is central to the four goals of the
liberal arts as well as the land-grant traditions, but there are barriers that obstruct the linking of elements into a community of
scholars. This section explores the barriers and frames the attitudes that might overcome them.

The past 150 years have seen the liberal arts college in a
research university such as the University of Wisconsin grow from
a small homogeneous enclave to a heterogeneous complexity of
many smaller communities. While it is always dangerous to look
back at some golden age of simplicity, it is obvious that today's
liberal arts college is populated by persons from more varied
backgrounds and with more varied goals than in the past; that the
number of subjects judged worthy to hold a place in the curriculum has exploded; and that this growth, worthy though it is, often
strains the coherence of the liberal arts college.

One cannot expect that the next 150 years will be less complex. *What serves as the link among such diverse elements? What*

makes all of this into one scholarly endeavor—a community of scholars?

Just as a large metropolitan area has many smaller communities from which its citizens draw their identity, so do large universities bring together many communities of scholars with common interests in research and teaching, common backgrounds, and common status as faculty, staff, or students. The community of scholars is first and foremost an intellectual community, and this will be discussed first. But it is more than that: it is a community of people, and this is the second topic to be explored.

Maintaining an intellectual community is indeed a challenge because of the barriers of specialization and the difficulties of communication. Specialization is an inevitable consequence of progress in research, but it almost precludes meaningful communication across disciplinary and even interdisciplinary boundaries.

Is it desirable to foster a larger community encompassing more specialized ones? It is, because in the future today's specialities will be mixed and swirled like so many paints on the artist's palette. Since no one can say how this might happen, communication among the many communities is vital. Also, the public—parents, citizens, public officials—needs to see the commonalities that link the various liberal arts communities, rather than the divisions. People are more likely to support an endeavor with a common purpose that transcends the intricate variety, and the liberal arts college must articulate this in a manner that is both accessible and accurate. After all, the goals of *education of the complete person* and *education for citizenship* are shams unless there is some common understanding within the liberal arts college about what its various components are all about. If the liberal arts college is simply an administrative construction to funnel resources into the specialties, it will not prevail.

The barriers to common understanding are high indeed. As the scholar scales ever higher peaks of knowledge, the valleys that reveal the common origins are often obscured by the clouds of details. Climbers are evermore separated from those on nearby peaks. From the lofty heights, profound connections between the various peaks can be discerned, but only if one has patience to wait for the clouds to dissipate. Furthermore, graduate students do not start in the valley, where they can appreciate the connections, but are airlifted to a spot near their own special peak, where they discover that what appears to be the summit in fact turns out to be the foothill of a still higher range.

This is exhilarating work, but it makes "a community of scholars" a romantic notion from the past. It takes time to descend to a level where climbers from other mountains can be met and experiences shared. Few will take the time.

This suggests the need for new breeds of scholars, those who delight at mid-altitudes, integrating and consolidating what has been achieved on related mountains, and those whose joy comes from maintaining the lush valleys of connectedness.

While communication within the scholarly community is hard, it is particularly difficult to communicate scholarly activities to an audience outside the university. Discussing research in depth requires a special language, and yet the scholar also has an obligation to explain his or her research to a wider community. Dean Mark H. Ingraham (L&S, 1942–61) deplored the inability of scientists and humanists to communicate across disciplines, not only with each other but with the general public. He wrote:

> Communication comes from shared ideas, shared emotions, and shared intellectual experience. . . . Of course, specialists will and should communicate with each other on the technical level, but scientists have also the obligation to communicate with the public. May I add that the poet has a greater (and I fear at the present an equally neglected) obligation to do so.

Communication is a prerequisite to common understanding, but of course it does not always result in that understanding.

Accessible discourse is not necessarily easy, and it requires commitment on the part of the listener, not just the speaker, to work hard in an area outside his or her own area of expertise.

Turning now from the intellectual underpinnings of a scholarly community to its human dimensions, three serious threats must be noted. The first is that for the liberal arts undergraduate, their academic lives will remain unconnected with their lives outside the classroom. The traditionally-aged student, fresh from high school, is passing through a time of tremendous personal development—becoming an adult, forming adult relationships with peers, establishing distance from parents and hometown, discovering a life meaning, choosing a career. Thus, there is more for students to accomplish than earning degrees. And yet, if the academic and nonacademic parts of students lives remain unconnected, they will have passed through the liberal arts college without truly becoming members of the community of scholars.

The second threat is the conflict between research and service. This conflict is much more real than the supposed contest between teaching and research. Rarely do the most prestigious faculty spend the time necessary to grasp internal problems of the university. The problems are too complex and the drive to maintain scholarly reputation is too great. It is becoming more difficult to fill committee rosters, and even to find qualified and willing faculty to be chairs of their departments. Thus, the infrastructure of shared governance that undergirds the broadest community of scholars is crumbling on many campuses, particularly those with a "bottom-up" tradition.

The third threat to the community is that the liberal arts college is too white and, in many disciplines, too male, especially among the faculty. While there is not any significant argument against the desirability of higher education reflecting the demographic make-up of the nation, there is great contentiousness over methods to accomplish this goal. In the 1960s methods were often articulated in terms of a "color-blind" or "gender-blind" society—that is, everyone is judged on his or her own merits without regard to skin color or gender. But who is going to do the judging except for the entrenched mainstream, white, male society? Thus, the color-blind approach forced the "others" to abandon their heritage and approaches and adopt those of the mainstream. Affirmative action was an attempt to create broader opportunities, but now the combined forces of a sense of fairness and a lack of progress threaten to undo the little progress that has been made.

The nation is foundering. The temptation for the liberal arts college is to sink back into a state of quiet acceptance of the status quo. After all, its record in the best of times was not great, and there are so many other pressing challenges. If this is the chosen course of (in)action, however, the community of scholars will be fatally flawed since the publicly perceived (and actual) chasm between academia and reality will steadily widen.

Thus, an important question to ask is: What defines a modern community of scholars? The past is not a true guide because the environment has changed too much. In truth, the past has been falsely glorified for its quiet harmony. To create a modern community of scholars does not mean that all scholars must become polymaths, experts in all fields. But it does mean that there needs to be a willingness to speak to one another in understandable terms without losing intellectual integrity, and it means that there must be an eagerness to listen. It means vigorous striving after knowledge, but with respect for and civility toward other scholars, and a profound respect for knowledge, all knowledge, itself. It means a willingness to do the hard and inglorious work of community building and maintenance. It means welcoming those who have been previously excluded and it means being willing to let their presence change the community itself. This is the challenge—not to re-create a lost community from the past, but to define the community of tomorrow.

The Challenge of Truth

Ye shall know the truth and the truth shall make you free.
—John 7:32

The quotation from the Gospel of John is on a plaque donated by the Class of 1955 and affixed to the outer wall of South Hall, the principal administrative building of the College of Letters and Science. The understanding of "truth" today is much more complex and tentative than it was in 1955. Is truth something to be found "out there," or is it a strict invention of the human intellect? If it is the latter, is there any truth at all? Does the "truth" make one free?

Liberal arts colleges are places where intelligent people experiment with ideas and try out new ways of viewing the world, where "What if" questions can be seriously discussed and the intellectual and philosophical consequences of tentative answers can be fully explored. Some of the questions and answers will become part of accepted knowledge; others will be set aside and not considered again. But the important point is that teachers and students have been able to think, experiment, write, and discuss their way through questions both significant and insignificant. This is serious and it is fun. One of the privileges and responsibilities of the liberal arts college is to explore "truth" within a relatively protected environment, where the discussions do not always have to make "sense" in accord with prevailing views of society at the moment.

In recent years, one position has been to assert that there is no such thing as "truth" in an absolute sense. Adherents to this view argue that "truth" is a construct developed within specific historical, social, and cultural contexts. This is true in fields ranging from literature (what is the true meaning of a Wordsworth poem?), to history (what really caused the Civil War?), and even into mathematics (is one geometry more valid than another?). In every field, the choice of research topics and accepted norms of discourse are controlled by the most influential members of the community, and this, it is claimed, makes it hopeless to determine the absolute truth or falsity of any assertion. Some argue that it is all a matter of who has the "power" to make certain "truths" stick.

It is, of course, a logical paradox to assert as a *truth* that there is *no* truth. Even if one does not take this position, there are many kinds of truth: there is the inductive truth of science, the deductive truth of mathematical reasoning, and the relative truth of humanistic and artistic interpretations.

The liberal arts cannot survive, however, unless a belief in truth survives. What does "education of the complete person" mean in the absence of truth? What does "life in a democracy" mean? What does "lifelong learning" mean? The notion that people are shaped by cultural, historical, and even linguistic assumptions and contexts does not mean that truth is impossible, but it does put certain—and perhaps not always utterly knowable—parameters on that truth. It means that ideas about truth are not necessarily transcendent, universal, true for all time, or even that they describe what really happened. It means that ideas about truth are inherently tentative.

The liberal arts are about the search for truth: for what really is, for what really happened, for what something really means. This is a never-ending quest because it is a human quest. The questions that are asked and the methods that are used will change significantly over time. Even the answers will change. Yet to be part of the liberal arts in the future is to agree to be part of the search, to be a member of the community of scholars. It means to try to understand what all the other members of the community are looking for as well. The poetic or artistic understanding of a sunset can stand co-equal to its scientific understanding; both have validity without co-opting each other's methodologies. All should be in the business of trying to understand. While mistakes will be made, distinctions improperly drawn, and evidence overlooked, all should agree that there is something out there worth looking for.

The Challenge of Academic Freedom

> Whatever may be the limitations which trammel inquiry
> elsewhere, we believe that the great State University of
> Wisconsin should ever encourage that continual and
> fearless sifting and winnowing by which alone the truth
> may be found.
>
> —Board of Regents, University of Wisconsin, 1894

For more than a hundred years, the students and faculty at the
University of Wisconsin–Madison have studied and learned under
the protection of the glorious statement of academic freedom
quoted above. This statement did not appear full-blown out of
the mists of a Lake Mendota morning. It appeared because some-
body thought that economics professor Richard Ely was advocat-
ing labor unions and indoctrinating students with dangerous
ideas.

Indoctrination—coercing students to accept a professor's
ideas—is not sanctioned by the sifting and winnowing statement.
But free inquiry by both students and faculty is.

In his recent essay, *The Limits of Academic Freedom*, City
University of New York English professor Louis Menand opens
with this line: "Coercion is natural; freedom is artificial . . . we
would not even have the concept of freedom if the reality of coercion were not present."

Thus, academic freedom, like all laws, has been set up as an
artificial system to protect scholars (students and faculty alike) in
their "fearless sifting and winnowing." Menand points out, however, that academic freedom is "*inherently* problematic."

What are some of the problems? One is that teaching and
learning are never value-free. This applies equally to the sciences
and to the humanities. Professors profess: they teach because they
believe in something and because they want to share their point
of view with their students. Academic freedom protects this incli-
nation. Likewise the teacher must give the student the freedom to

question and ultimately not accept. This give-and-take is where the learning occurs.

But there are always grades and academic standards. The teacher ultimately decides what is acceptable and what isn't, whether it is a proof in geometry or an interpretation of a sonnet of Shakespeare.

Grading is not coercion, but intolerance by the teacher is. This is one reason why grade appeal procedures have been established, so that a broader group of faculty can judge the propriety of what has occurred. This is not coercion either, but a responsive way to protect the learning environment.

A second intrinsic problem with academic freedom is that it is related to, but distinct from, freedom of speech. Freedom of speech is a constitutional right of every American. But every institution has the obligation to establish internal rules to further its mission. All rules limit freedoms. For example, every business has the right to require its employees to be courteous to its customers. This limits the employees' freedom of speech. A university is not a business, students are not customers, and universities should have a high tolerance for divergent points of view. A university should not only tolerate but *encourage* a divergence of viewpoints for both faculty and students.

Thus, a university has the obligation to establish rules to protect academic freedom. But, as has been discussed, the university also has an obligation to nurture a diverse community of scholars and to establish rules to guard against behaviors and practices that undermine this community. This rule-setting can be interpreted by some as tyranny. As the eighteenth-century philosopher Montesquieu wrote in *The Spirit of the Laws*, book 19: "There are two types of tyranny; one tangible emanates from violent governments; the other is the tyranny of opinion, which is felt when those who want to rule establish a state of affairs that is shocking to the manner of thoughts of others."

For some students, faculty, and staff, the "mainstream culture" of the university constitutes a tyranny of the first kind. They contend that the rules of the university inherently exclude classes of people, or make the learning environment inhospitable. Others, usually members of the mainstream, consider rules to govern offensive speech, which were established to foster a hospitable environment, to be tyranny of the second type.

There is some validity in both positions, but as often formulated they are mutually reinforcing delusions. It is not tyranny at work here but rather two values: freedom of speech and the goal of an open community. The Constitution gives favor to the former, which can be used not only to create dissension but also to create dialogue. Contention often results, because speech so easily offends, but the goal of even contentious dialogue should be to strengthen the community.

A third problem for liberal arts colleges these days is the controversy over "political correctness." Much has been written about this topic, often to the detriment of public understanding. The very concept should be foreign to the university, suggesting as it does that "political power," rather than the power of ideas and persuasion, dominates scholarly discourse. Of course, some outrageous acts have been committed and some outrageous assertions have been made on all sides. But the surface discourse results from the tectonic movements along the fault lines of truth, diversity, and academic freedom. A major challenge for the liberal arts college is to bring harmony to this troubled area.

This is a serious issue for liberal arts colleges because "political correctness," "tenured radicals," and other epithets refer to them specifically and not to the professional schools. Those without and within the university who lament attention being given to cultural studies, ethnic studies, and women's studies are criticizing the liberal arts. Those who feel that their freedom of speech is curtailed by university rules that force them to be "sensitive" are largely in the liberal arts, as are their antagonists. These controversies will not be settled in the court of law, where fact and reason prevail, but in the court of public opinion, where rhetoric and anecdote rule.

The problem of truth has already been discussed, as has the issue of diversity. As the backgrounds of those who participate in higher education—both as students and as faculty—become more varied, it is inevitable that fields of study represented within the university will become more varied. Who will decide which fields flourish and which will be banished? Without a sense of community, and without a common understanding of truth, it is impossible to predict the answer. Academic freedom is a guide; is it also the determinant?

A fourth intrinsic problem with academic freedom is that its development has accompanied, and now protects, academic specialization. Academic freedom allows faculty who have received appropriate credentials from their peers in their specialty to continue to pursue their interests.

The power of the process of certification should not be underestimated. Consider the career path of a stereotypical scholar-in-the-making: early interest, sustained by stimulating teachers in high school; excellent undergraduate experience enriched by undergraduate research; admission to a "top 10" graduate program to study under the tutelage of a leader in the field and a thesis topic in one of the hottest areas of research. Then comes a faculty position at a top-flight university, then early success in getting grants, attracting graduate students, and building a scholarly program. The budding scholar chooses a research topic different enough from previous experiences to establish independence and yet close enough so that rapid progress can be made. After hard work for six years, putting career ahead of everything else, being lucky, achieving success, publishing, receiving invitations to speak at prestigious institutions and conferences, comes tenure, which carries the right to continue doing the same, striving to reach the pinnacle, reaching full professor, being recognized as one of the few top leaders in the field, helping define the problems that are most significant for others to work on.

This is an extreme characterization perhaps, but not unrecognizable. Its repetition over the past half-century has created a faculty that is extremely successful, extremely specialized, and extremely conservative (in an academic sense). This group excels in what it does, which is often very fine indeed. The system is well designed to perpetuate a set of standards and activities. It is very stable. But if the system needs to change—by including people with nonstandard backgrounds or fields of study that are not part of the system— then change is very slow and difficult, not because the individuals in it are unimaginative or mean-spirited, but because the mores of scholarship have been so completely internalized over the years.

Thus, academic freedom does not inherently foster respect and civility between one specialty and another. A discipline-based academic freedom does not inherently cause the historian to respect the sociologist or the economist to respect the political scientist. Nor does it encourage those well-established disciplines to respect newly-emerged fields of inquiry such as women's studies, ethnic studies, global studies, and a host of interdisciplinary programs now on the intellectual landscape.

Academic freedom supports the autonomy of scholars and disciplines, but it does not inherently strengthen the university as an academic community. Discipline-based academic freedom must be leavened by healthy doses of humility, tolerance, and respect for different approaches to knowledge.

The Challenge of Relevance

If the *people* feel education to be their greatest want, why are colleges begging from door to door . . . Somewhere, along the electric chain which binds the different classes of community together, the laborer at his plough, to the thinker in his silent study, there are rusted links. The relation between industry and intellectual cultivation is lost sight of, and this is the true reason why colleges are petitioners for the patronage they ought to command.

—Ezra Carr, first professor of chemistry at the University of Wisconsin; spoken to the Board of Regents in 1856.

Members of liberal arts faculties often take offense at pressures to make their subjects "relevant," and well they should. Short-term, superficial relevance is not the subject of this essay. The value of studying Shakespeare, or medieval art history, or cosmology, or theoretical economics, or abstract mathematics should not be questioned. These are glories of the human mind that liberal arts colleges have a duty both to protect and exalt. The rusted links that Ezra Carr decried were those that should link the community of scholars to the wider community. The liberal arts must not lose sight of this broader relevance: They must do *useful work* if their future is to be assured.

This chapter has focused so far on issues mostly internal to the university. Ignored have been such crucial issues, seemingly external to higher education, as world population trends, economic disparity, ethnicity and democracy, health care, public safety, national defense, public confidence in government, environmental stewardship, the nation's deteriorating infrastructure, dwindling supplies of nonrenewable energy resources, consequences of increasing life spans, expansion and application of technology (especially health care technology and information technology), and maintaining a healthy economy. These are monumental issues whose resolution will profoundly affect higher education, but over which universities have no direct control. Graduates of liberal arts colleges, however, will be involved in resolving these issues, which gives added weight to the future of the liberal arts.

Education in the liberal arts has persisted throughout Western history during times when the future looked equally daunting. Perhaps the most profound external influence on the liberal arts in the immediate future will be the public's attitude toward learning. In the 1990s there are significant forces working against the liberal arts—from public policy that puts public safety, defense, and health care ahead of public education, to personal goals that put credentials ahead of learning. Even so, it is difficult to believe that the liberal arts, which provide the broadest base for understanding an unfolding future, will be pushed from the center of higher education. But to stay in that position, the liberal arts must continue to do useful work.

What is the useful work that the liberal arts college must do to remain relevant to students, to colleagues, and to the public— to establish the relation between industry and intellectual cultivation?

The useful work of the faculty with regard to students is to encourage an attitude of lifelong learning. Someone has said that education is what is left over after the student has forgotten all that has been learned. Many puzzles will be encountered by the liberal arts graduate after graduation that are not explicitly encountered in any course. So the question for the faculty is: After your students have forgotten the details of what you taught them, what will they take with them to enrich and guide their lives in a search for truth?

If you have taught them a course about the Civil War, will they be able to use historical analysis to inform present understanding, even though they have forgotten the details of battles? If you have taught them a chemistry course, will they be able to approach environmental problems with intelligence, even though they have to look up the elemental form of nitrogen. If you have taught them a course in nineteenth-century art history, will your students have a lifelong interest in art, even if they sometimes forget the difference between Manet and Monet? If you have taught them introductory economics, will they be able to sort through conflicting approaches to inflation and unemployment, even though they have to review the details of economic theory?

This is not to suggest that the goal of the college graduate is just to understand superficially without the background of facts and basic theories. Rather, a goal of the liberal arts is to instill the capacity for lifelong learning.

The focus on lifelong learning also suggests that some faculty will devote time to making the university accessible to the non-traditional student through distance education and instructional technology. Surely, there is nothing to replace the personal, face-to-face interaction between student and teacher within a residential college, but for a growing number of students of all ages a liberal arts education in another medium is the only option. This should never become the core of the liberal arts, but it can become a useful adjunct.

The focus on education for a productive life means that faculty are concerned about the transition of the liberal arts student to the world of work. The challenge is to offer legitimate work-related learning experiences for students before they graduate, through internships and volunteer experiences, or to provide transitional programs that follow the baccalaureate degree. Not only will students be enriched by such experiences, and their liberal arts degrees will become more immediately useful, but the faculty will become more fully aware of and engaged in the useful work they can do outside the university.

This is not a trivial suggestion. As John Dewey wrote in *Experience and Education*: "There is one permanent frame of reference: namely, the organic connection between education and personal experience. . . . [But] the belief that all genuine education comes about through experience does not mean that all experiences are genuinely or equally educative." Thus, creating useful "personal experiences" for liberal arts students requires an academic investment to create and evaluate those experiences. Consider, for example, an internship program that gives academic credit for French majors to work for a year in biotechnology companies in France. How is the experience to be vetted as worthwhile by academic standards? Do the principles of academic freedom extend to such an experience in the same way as they apply to campus courses? Is it appropriate for faculty to do the necessary work to make the contacts to initiate and sustain the program? Should the program be part of the undergraduate degree or part of a transitional master's program? Does it have to be academically-related at all? These are examples of the hard questions that have to be answered to extend education beyond the campus boundaries.

The focus on education for citizenship means that the liberal arts college encourages students to participate as citizens both in the university and in the world at large. For some students in some majors, this may mean academic credit, but for many others it simply means an acknowledgment of legitimacy. Movements are underway to break down the artificial walls between the academic and nonacademic parts of a student's life. Moving academic programs into student dormitories is one example. Facilitating student volunteerism is another. Creating collaborative learning and team approaches to problem-solving is a third. Although not always stated explicitly, these movements build citizenship. They increase the capacity of people to work together for a common purpose. As with all fledgling movements, they are led by the dedicated few. Moving them into the mainstream will be difficult, but it is useful work because it will increase the value of the liberal arts experience to the student and to society.

Doing useful work for colleagues means collaborating in research, teaching courses of use to other departments, supporting interdisciplinary endeavors, and participating in shared governance. More and more, it will mean collaborations with colleagues at other institutions in order to share limited resources of faculty, students, and equipment.

Some service work is easy; other work is much more difficult, given the limited time most faculty can spare for service. It is naturally more appealing to be asked to chair a national professional task force than it is to chair a campus committee. Service as department chair is always seen as dictating a hiatus from research, and thus more and more faculty eschew what used to be a high honor bestowed by one's colleagues. The local has a hard time competing with the national, which is both understandable and injurious to the health of the liberal arts college.

Collaborating in research is usually easy; collaborating in teaching is often difficult. To support more interdisciplinary teaching, liberal arts colleges must become more clever in removing barriers, whether they be at the departmental or the institutional level. Collaborating on maintaining and updating the curriculum is another activity that attracts few faculty.

Doing useful work for the public is critical for the health of the liberal arts. Some faculty do this quite naturally as an integral part of their academic interests. The leader of the marching band, the members of the public policy institute, the faculty in urban and regional planning—they are all on the front lines, visible to the public. Not as visible, perhaps, but of even more pervasive importance, are the research contributions of many faculty, graduate students, undergraduates, and postdoctoral fellows. A high-technology, global economy is a direct result of university-based research, much of it in the fundamental areas of the natural and social sciences. The humanities and arts also play an important role in helping U.S. businesses to understand other cultures.

The research of other faculty appears to be more remote, but only superficially. In human relationships it is often asserted that "six degrees of separation" are all that is required to link any one person to any other in the world. (This concept has recently been modeled by mathematicians, using two different types of lattice, either structured or random, and introducing shortcuts that dramatically illustrate how a big world can be turned into a small world.) A shopkeeper in Kansas is linked to her pastor who is linked to her seminary professor who is linked to a missionary in India who is linked to a shopkeeper in that country—four degrees of separation. Six degrees are entirely too many to link any faculty member's work with the general public. The abstract mathematician teaches calculus to the engineer who develops the transistor that transforms society. The international relations specialist gets an internship in Washington for a graduate student who goes on to become Secretary of State. The English professor edits an anthology that establishes the canon for African-American literature. The implications of the work of a communications researcher unexpectedly puts her into the middle of the fray over television ratings. Few liberal arts faculty members are separated by more than two degrees from a positive impact on the public;

that is, they are doing useful work.

Finally, the liberal arts do useful work for the professions. Lawyers, doctors and other health professionals, teachers, engineers, business people, researchers of every stripe—they all receive a foundation in the liberal arts. Faculty collaborations between the liberal arts and the professions enrich both. There are few great professional schools that are not in a relationship with a great liberal arts college. This is the environment for useful work.

The Future of the Liberal Arts

Change? Yes, we must change, only show me the Theory, and I will be at the barricades, show me the book of the next Beautiful Theory, and I promise you these blind eyes will see again, just to read it, to devour that text. Show me the words that will reorder the world, or else keep silent. If the snake sheds his skin before a new skin is ready he will be naked in the world, prey to the forces of chaos. Without his skin he will be dismantled, lose coherence and die. Have you, my little serpents, a new skin?

> Words spoken by Aleksii Antelluvianovich Prelapsarianov, the World's Oldest Living Bolshevik, in the play *Angels in America, Part II: Perestroika*, by Tony Kushner (1993 Pulitzer Prize for Drama)

To know the narrative in advance is to turn yourself into a machine. What makes humans human is precisely that they do not know the future. That is why they do the fateful and amusing things they do: who can say how anything will turn out? Therein lies the only hope for redemption, discovery, and—let's be frank—fun, fun, fun! . . . But you do not have to know in order to see what stories your life's efforts will bring you. The mystery is all.

> From "People Like That Are the Only People Here," by Professor Lorrie Moore (UW–Madison Creative Writing Program), *New Yorker*, January 27, 1997

The final section of this chapter discusses the future of the liberal arts, but it will not produce "the next Beautiful Theory" to govern liberal arts programs in the next period of history. One cannot expect to produce the "words that will reorder the world" overnight; people will not move from one Theory to the next without much discussion and debate. It is a fearful task to question a skin that has served so well for the last forty years at least. The excellence of the liberal arts is unquestioned, but the forces of chaos threaten, and keeping the old skin too long brings its own dangers. Thus, to start and to some extent frame the debate does not preordain the outcome. The goal is to call forth the wisdom, insight, and creativity of the liberal arts community to create a vision of a common future.

The twentieth century has been good to higher education. A century ago, guided by the principles of *specialization* of the individual scholar and *production of knowledge* (research and its applications) as primary goals of the faculty, the great public research universities were founded.

At Wisconsin, John Bascom's presidency saw the beginnings of the research university and the Wisconsin Idea. The presidency of Charles R. Adams saw the Ely trial and the famous statement of academic freedom now affixed to the wall of Bascom Hall. Following Adams, Bascom's student Charles R. Van Hise refined the concept of the Wisconsin Idea and further developed the research capacity of the university. These developments took nearly forty-five years, from 1874 when Bascom came west to Wisconsin to the end of Van Hise's presidency in 1918. When Bascom took over, UW–Madison was a small college in the Midwest; when Van Hise left, it was a national research university.

The innovations that created the emerging research universities brought dramatic changes in the late nineteenth-century colleges, and replaced the model of faculty member as generalist (preserver) and transmitter (teacher) of knowledge. They also changed colleges from local institutions primarily occupied with the concerns of the region to universities with national scope.

From the perspective of time, these changes may seem natural, occurring in the course of orderly evolution. Not so; they were controversial and they took time to become established. The Ely Trial, which gave rise to the "sifting and winnowing" statement is well known, but not as well known are these words of frustration written by John Bascom as he left Madison to return to the east: "I leave the University of Wisconsin simply because I have had no sufficient liberty in doing my work."

Despite contentious beginnings, research universities have produced generations of leaders in business, government, science, the arts, and academia. Today, Wisconsin remains among the handful of public universities that can claim national prominence in teaching, research, and service. Specialization and research have amply repaid the public investment in higher education.

The second period of growth for research universities was fueled first by the GIs returning from World War II, and then by their sons and daughters who doubled enrollments over just a few years in the 1960s, just as enrollments had doubled during the Van Hise presidency. The nation in the 1950s and 60s had five main reasons to invest heavily in higher education:

- to provide access to a better life for a generation robbed of opportunity by the Depression and World War II, and to their children;
- to further support the kind of research that created the atom bomb and showed how science can be used in the defense of the nation;
- to build up both the social sciences, (in order to help understand how to deal with the nation's domestic and international problems), and the biological sciences (in order to ensure the health of its citizens);
- to win the race to the moon;
- to win the Cold War.

At this time, too, federal support for the humanities and the arts was introduced through the creation of the National Endowment for the Humanities and the National Endowment for the Arts. This legislation recognized society's need for meaning, communication, creative expression, and the general enrichment of life and knowledge that characterize work in the humanities and arts. In Wisconsin, there were additional factors: the enormous success of the Wisconsin Idea in making the university relevant to the people of Wisconsin, and the cultural heritage of Wisconsin people, who valued learning beyond what one might expect for an agricultural state of modest resources.

All factors came together to produce a consensus for education and research. They formed the basis for an unwritten contract between the government and the universities, which called for the government to support higher education in return for the universities' responsiveness to the needs of the state and nation.

Looking back, it appears that the changes that occurred after World War II were natural and flowed without dissent. Again, this was not so. Critics at that time decried a diminution of attention to undergraduate education. Others worried about a loss of academic integrity, which they viewed as the result of the partnership of research universities with the federal government. But the forces for change were too strong.

Liberal arts colleges within major research universities have prospered in this environment of growth. At times referred to as "the teaching college of UW–Madison," the College of Letters and Science (L&S) has, as noted earlier, traditionally taught 95 percent of all freshman-sophomore credits and awarded about 55 percent of all undergraduate degrees. The quality of its faculty, instructional academic staff, and teaching assistants has been (and is) superb. Teaching also encompasses graduate-level teaching. L&S has traditionally produced about 45 percent of the master's and almost 50 percent of the doctorate degrees awarded at UW–Madison each year, and its faculty have been (and are) exemplary teachers and mentors of graduate students.

Its teaching role goes hand in hand with the fact that L&S is one of the premier research colleges of the university, both in terms of funded research (L&S is second only to the Medical School in total federal research funding), largely in the natural and social sciences, and unfunded research, largely in the humanities and the arts. An environment of outstanding scholarship and research provides a climate of intellectual stimulation for all students, both undergraduate and graduate. They are in fact symbiotic activities, and L&S has excelled in both.

The excellence of L&S has resulted from strong adherence to the principle that "excellence attracts excellence." Two-thirds of L&S departments can lay reasonable claim to being among the "top ten" research and graduate education departments in their discipline, nationwide, and nearly all are among the top twenty. Since preeminence in research and scholarship is based on the quality of the faculty, recruiting, nurturing, and retaining an excellent faculty has been a top priority of L&S. Not only does the graduate program depend on this, but the excellence of the undergraduate program depends on a scholarly faculty.

With such a distinguished history, why should L&S have to worry about its future? It remains in fine scholarly shape. Significant new energy has been devoted over the past ten years by the faculty in undergraduate education, and research activities remain healthy. Beneath the surface, however, none of the factors that supported growth during the "golden era" of research universities is valid today. *Not one!* The prerequisites for growth have disappeared, seemingly overnight, but in reality over the last twenty-five years. Consider:

- enrollments will not double again over a short time span;
- for too many students, college is no longer an opportunity to have a better life than their parents; it is a method to get job credentials that are essential just to keep up;
- commercial and political misuses of scientific discovery often loom larger in the nation's thinking than the overwhelming successes that still flow from university laboratories;
- Congress is turning away from federal intervention to solve domestic and international problems;

- except in health-related areas—a significant exception—there are no large-scale science and engineering projects that capture the public's imagination in the same way that the race to the moon did;
- the Cold War has ended, and with it the national defense rationale for federal support of scientific research, language training, and area studies;
- Congress has imposed significant cuts on the National Endowment for the Humanities and the National Endowment for the Arts.

In addition, the public seems to have less and less confidence in *any* institution, be it the Presidency, Congress, business, the arts, or state and local government. Unfairly, public research universities are often included on this unfortunate list. "Faculty bashing" seems to be a national pastime among political and business leaders. Even as good economic times have returned to the U.S., and Wisconsin finds itself with a budget surplus, higher education has to compete with many other compelling demands for state resources. The environment for public higher education is greatly changed from that in the "golden era."

Higher education should not have to go begging for support. A college degree is still key to a productive life. Research universities offer a uniquely rich undergraduate experience. They also train the future professoriate for all of higher education, and conduct the vast majority of research in the nation, especially fundamental research. This research and scholarly activity in the humanities and arts, in the social sciences, and in the natural sciences provides the intellectual capital for the future of the nation.

Educational leaders eloquently articulate these values of higher education. If eloquence and truth controlled the political allocation of resources, higher education would continue to enjoy the support it so richly deserves. Even politicians sympathetic to the value of higher education are caught in powerful forces to reduce taxes and increase funding for prisons. Even within the decreasing slice of public funding reserved for education, the problems of K–12 education seem more compelling than those of colleges and universities.

Educators must be realistic. They must use all of the observational and analytical skills at their collective disposal to accurately assess the situation. They must also make assumptions and choices. For example, they might assume that today's diminished public support is a passing thing and that higher education will soon return to the golden years. Or, they can perhaps more realistically assume that the future environment for higher education will be substantially different from the past. Evidence provided by current trends, as well as prudence in planning for the future, force the latter assumption. However, given that assumption, one can still choose between an optimistic or pessimistic view of the future. Although the future environment may be different, it can also be better if liberal arts colleges gain control over their own future. If they find a way to continue to prosper in research and teaching they will remain wonderful places to lead an academic life. It is not sufficient, however, to rail against current public misconceptions or decry the lack of understanding of the importance of the liberal arts.

Both realism and optimism imply *change*. And just as the changes initiated in the nineteenth century and in the mid-twentieth century were controversial, changes required to transform the liberal arts college within a research university will also be controversial.

Understanding the past is difficult; predicting the future is close to impossible. What conditions that exist now and that will likely exist in the near future will have an impact on higher education? What new forces are developing with major implications for the future? It is imperative to analyze these conditions carefully and wisely. Liberal arts colleges can provide leadership for society about what the changing landscapes will require of higher education.

The past has been characterized by an expanding academic economy. An expanding economy supports research, which drives the growth of knowledge. The growth of knowledge demands specialization. Specialization supports the individual entrepreneur. An expanding economy allows the institution to support many specialties and thus avoid difficult choices between them.

The growth of knowledge always demands an expanding faculty, and an expanding academic economy supports it. In the 1960s, the two elements of increasing enrollments and increased federal support for research happily combined to support both the growth of faculty and the growth of knowledge.

Today there is a contracting academic economy. The compelling reasons for growth, or at least maintenance, in the size of the faculty are still present, but the financial support is not adequate. An awful imbalance exists between the growth of knowledge and the resources to cope with that growth. The well-balanced system that evolved in the 1960s is no more, and it is time to invent a new one. This will demand creativity, collegiality, and optimism. And it will require significant changes.

Significant change is extraordinarily difficult for any institution that has experienced great success in an expanding academic economy. Significant change does not have to mean either/or, but rather a balancing of:

- research and teaching priorities;
- specialization and individual entrepreneurship;
- competition versus cooperation;
- loyalty to the national profession versus loyalty to the local institution.

Asking the questions must not be seen as dictating the answers; that will only serve to freeze the mind. Much is to be gained by a reexamination of the commitments that drive the liberal arts and a formulation of a new sense of shared values that have a chance of providing flexibility, incentive for change, and continued excellence in research and teaching.

The magnitude of the changes that might be required to assure a bright future also have the potential of destroying excellence. This is particularly so if change is approached with the techniques of the past. *Liberal arts colleges must strive to avoid the trap of narrowly defining their choices as budget and management issues; rather, they should strive to set their planning within the intellectual and academic context of a vision of what it means to be a liberal arts college with a major teaching and research mission.*

Change is risky; once high quality and reputation are lost, they cannot easily be recovered. But the environment for liberal arts education in the 1990s will not preserve excellence unless there is change. Is the status quo an option? Is it not better to gamble on innovation to create a new path to continued excellence rather than to bet that the successful model of the last fifty years will ensure continued success in a much-changed environment? Here are five areas to guide a reexamination of the liberal arts in order to provide a context for change. Each of these points is made to suggest ways to approach change with courage and creativity rather than with fear and resentment.

1. Scholarship

Deep scholarship often requires a concentrated and piercing gaze at a narrow subject. Scholarship has come to mean total immersion in a chosen field of inquiry, and many faculty, staff, and graduate students have made magnificent contributions to the body of knowledge in this way. Yet, since public liberal arts colleges are wedded to the common good, they must address the needs of the larger society for transmission and integration of knowledge. Today's problems often require complex solutions that do not respect the boundaries of academic disciplines. Today's specialized faculty and the students they produce must learn to move beyond the boundaries of their expertise and interact with other experts to solve complex problems.

The future does not require that all scholars adopt the style of the Renaissance man or woman, abandoning their concentration in their chosen subspecialties to spread their efforts more widely but perhaps more thinly. Specialization will always be needed to advance knowledge and provide the foundation for integration. But there is a need to broaden the concept of worthwhile scholarship to include consolidating what is known, relating what is known in one field to what is known in another, and making specialized knowledge accessible to a broader audience. The descriptors "consolidation, transmission, application, and preservation" of knowledge need to be valued alongside "production and application." With a broadened concept of scholarship, the liberal arts stand the best chance of garnering the public support so vital to excellence.

The immediate future offers a unique opportunity to revitalize the American system of higher education with new ideas and new blood. This opportunity must not be muffed. The time is right to rethink scholarship and graduate education to assure its continued pertinence to the needs of both research and teaching institutions. The call for broader and more integrative scholarship has implications not only for how faculty pursue their own educational objectives but for how they prepare the graduate students who will be key members of the next generation of the professoriate.

2. Teaching

During the next five years, demographics predict that the number of undergraduates will *increase* while the number of graduate students will *decrease*. Given these probabilities, liberal arts colleges within major research universities may not be able to maintain excellence in undergraduate and graduate programs without significant changes to how they conceive of and deliver the undergraduate and graduate curriculum. A drop in graduate enrollments, for example, will make it difficult to sustain the richness of graduate offerings. A drop in the number of graduate students qualified to be teaching assistants can also have a profound effect on the undergraduate curriculum.

It is an unpleasant but simple arithmetical calculation that if the number of faculty and staff remains the same or decreases, and if the number of students increases, the student-teacher ratio will go up. This means that faculty and staff will have increased teaching obligations. They will either teach larger classes or more classes.

The student-teacher ratio, when averaged over all courses in a department, obscures a great deal of flexibility, however, since departments and programs have a great deal of control over the profile of class size. A modest increase in the ratio does not force the abolition of small classes, for example. Departments and programs also control their curricula and the way they engage their students. This is where the excitement of teaching lies and where creative change can occur.

If the future dictates a somewhat larger student-teacher ratio, the ability to teach in several areas of the undergraduate curriculum is one possible protector of research and graduate education. In some departments, all faculty are able to teach any undergraduate course. Others maintain a tradition of individual faculty "ownership" of courses. In many departments there is a mixture of the two extremes. If the number of graduate students declines while the number of undergraduates increases, the creation of more integrative courses could enable the faculty to serve increased numbers of undergraduates without increasing teaching load. More integrative courses also have value in their own right.

Teaching changes may occur by other means. Information technology and distance education present speculative new possibilities that might significantly change instruction, but probably not on the scale that its more avid adherents predict. Speculation about the growth of distance education should cause liberal arts colleges, however, to articulate the reasons why a residential experience should always remain the core experience for undergraduates. At the graduate level, information technology holds real promise in allowing collaborations among research universities to preserve critical enrollments in key graduate courses and to enhance collaboration across long distances.

3. Curriculum

The curriculum is the highest expression of the academic knowledge and values of the faculty. *Curriculum* means all of the many courses available to students; *curriculum* means general education requirements; *curriculum* means the requirements for certificates and majors.

The liberal arts curriculum is rich indeed. It reflects the scholarly achievements of the faculty. It may also reflect the specialization of the faculty and a strange incuriosity about overall educational purposes. Students need to be broadly acquainted with the main areas of intellectual thought and with their methods of inquiry. Thus, the ways in which the curriculum is conceived need to be examined. A commitment to the liberal arts means a commitment to explore new ways of engaging students.

For at least a century the research interests of the faculty have driven the curriculum. They teach what they have discovered. They are passing the fruits of inquiry along. But teaching also informs research. Mendeleev discovered the periodic table of the elements by trying to organize a general chemistry course and thereby laid the foundation for modern chemistry. Political science was created not because of a body of systematic political knowledge but because of a desire to create one in order to prepare students for democratic citizenship. Women's studies, multicultural studies, area studies, neurobiology, and other "interdisciplinary" programs are all attempts to extract a core of knowledge from a variety of disciplines and teach it from a different perspective. And from teaching will come further stimulation for research and scholarly activity.

There is now a need to make a thorough appraisal of whether the curriculum serves the values of the liberal arts: How can graduates be educated as responsible and productive citizens? Are they broadly educated with a lifelong love of learning? Is it possible that this examination of educational goals will contribute to the direction of research agendas?

4. Students

Through the curriculum, the liberal arts remain committed to the intellectual development of students, both undergraduate and graduate. While the college years are a period of significant personal growth for students, it is also likely to be the only significant opportunity for concentrated scholarly study in the student's life. It is an opportunity that must not be missed.

New technologies hold the potential for transforming the way in which students learn. "The classroom" even now is sometimes a computer screen wired to the Internet. An unanswered question is whether this development will move beyond "information transfer" into true learning. But liberal arts faculty are already at work on answering the critical question.

Outside the "classroom," liberal arts colleges are committed to providing academic support to undergraduates, including academic advising and career counseling, enrichment programs, and nonclassroom learning experiences for students. Academic advising helps students identify their interests, develop an educational plan, explore the intellectual resources of the campus, and develop career goals that are linked to their undergraduate experiences.

Liberal arts colleges must also remain committed to access. Most liberal arts colleges are in an excellent position to teach "the best and the brightest" who are already motivated to learn, and the faculty has a special mission to offer a challenging education to them. But the commitment to access must be more than this. Liberal arts colleges also should also reach out to students who have not yet discovered a motivation to learn, or who find themselves in a culture alien to their previous learning styles. This does not mean a lowering of academic standards, but rather development of innovative approaches to stimulate the nontraditional student.

The increasing diversity of the student body will require a multiplicity of teaching and learning methods. Technology will offer increased flexibility of delivery and enhanced content. Special undergraduate research programs, revitalized honors programs, and small group interactions must continue as an integral part of the pursuit of a liberal arts education. Specialized learning centers can enhance opportunities for students with unique talents. Residential colleges, such as the Chadbourne Residential College, can offer opportunities to students for citizenship, leadership, and interaction with both faculty and visiting professionals.

5. The Organization of the Liberal Arts

Within the liberal arts colleges, there are already those who wish to re-create a community of scholars who can link their specialized knowledge to work together to address important intellectual issues. Some of the most exciting intellectual advances are made in areas such as biophysics or biomedical engineering, areas that cut across traditional departmental and even school and college boundaries. Just as the natural sciences fought to become an accepted part of the liberal arts in the nineteenth century, and the social sciences in the twentieth, so too are emerging disciplines fighting to gain a foothold in the rich soil of the liberal arts.

Liberal arts colleges are mainly organized around tenure-granting departments. The number of departments has increased since World War II, partly due to subdisciplines within a department striking out to form their own disciplines, and partly due to "interdisciplinary" programs becoming "disciplinary" departments. If, in the ongoing process of change, the established tenure-granting departments use their power over faculty appointments to rigidly protect existing intellectual boundaries, the liberal arts of the future will be impoverished.

Finally, and most significantly, liberal arts colleges need to think about strategies for hiring and retaining faculty. A bottom-up approach works well in an expanding economy. If there is a vacancy, the appropriate faculty group gets together to choose the subdiscipline most desirable to that subgroup. That works when *adding* to an academic area or maintaining the status quo. In a contracting economy, if colleges are forced to *lose* academic sub-specialties, they should examine whether a more organized and self-conscious approach is required.

If the liberal arts are to move to a broader conception of learning and knowing, if they are going to encourage more of their faculty to move beyond narrow research specialization and try new approaches that cross conventional boundaries, it just may be that they will have to challenge, at times, the established standards and prestige systems of the national disciplinary professions. This is a horrifying thought. Prestigious liberal arts colleges avidly await the latest national reputational rankings of graduate and undergraduate programs; they diligently total their annual proceeds in extramural research grants; they annually score the faculty on their ability to publish in nationally refereed journals. Any suggestion that this might cause distortions in the liberal arts mission immediately opens the questioner to charges of not adhering to high standards.

This is not an either/or choice. Liberal arts colleges have both national responsibilities to the professions and local responsibilities to students and to the public. But both responsibilities raise questions about how to maintain balance in a contracting economy.

When one reads the history of the College of Letters and Science, one discovers that many of the achievements that have brought it distinction in the past did *not* come from imitating academic fashions elsewhere. Bascom did not try to duplicate the elitist approach to graduate education promulgated by Johns Hopkins. Turner was emphatically not following what was being done in history at Harvard. Ely and Commons were not "contributing" to what was then accepted as the prestigious orthodoxy in political economy; rather, they were in open rebellion against it.

If liberal arts colleges choose to be leaders on their own terms, the leadership will come from within departments and from tenure committees that are willing to use their own judgment in making recruitment and retention decisions, judging faculty across disciplinary boundaries, and asking impertinent questions about the value of specialized scholarship to common educational goals. But before this contentious and frightening line of thought can be pursued further, a consensus about common goals must be reached.

This chapter initiates a discussion; it does not provide answers. The discussion will be *hard work*. One cannot expect a distinguished group of faculty and staff, who have been trained as specialists, who have made significant contributions, and who have won accolades for theses accomplishments to step back easily and consider how a system in which they have excelled might have to change. But this is exactly what must happen.

Appendix: Predictions

> The further we try to project into the future, the more certain it is that some unforeseen, perhaps unforeseeable discovery will shuffle the deck before we get there. . . . People who are otherwise intelligent are inclined to take . . . futurists seriously. The further ahead these "experts" project their minds, the deeper their insights are thought to be. If they think far enough ahead into the future, they're called "visionaries." . . . Futurists tell people what they want to hear—predictions that resonate with their own hopes, or fears, or religious convictions—and they make it interesting.
>
> —Robert L. Park, University of Maryland Professor of Physics

Faced with these critical remarks, anyone would be reluctant to say too much about the future of the liberal arts. Certainly, since safety resides in generalities, details should be omitted from any predictions. With some trepidation, therefore, twelve predictions are offered in conclusion and without justification as a time capsule to be opened by some curious soul in the future.

- The liberal arts tradition will survive although it will be modified by both internal and external forces.

- The frontier mentality (expansion is inevitable; individual goals prevail over common goals) will be replaced by a community mentality.
- The intellectual landscape of the liberal arts will evolve at an increasing rate; classical boundaries will become more permeable to interdisciplinary programs; new disciplines will appear.
- The main undergraduate liberal arts experience will continue to be on residential campuses.
- The undergraduate student body will increasingly divide into "rich" and "poor," reflecting the fragmentation of the middle class.
- Graduate education and research will continue to be an essential component in the entire liberal arts enterprise; research experiences will continue to be integrated into the undergraduate experience.
- The liberal arts community will become increasingly diverse in reflection of the larger society; this will be driven by economic forces, rather than philosophical or altruistic forces.
- The tenure system will crumble, not because of external attacks, but because it will no longer serve the faculty's needs for personal and professional freedom.
- Approaches to student learning will become more varied; the traditional lecture will not disappear but other modalities will become established.
- Basic communication and quantitative reasoning courses will continue to be the bedrock of a liberal arts education.
- New instructional technologies will be integrated into the learning experience, but no "revolution" will take place.
- Internationalization of the curriculum will continue; biology will expand; Greek and Latin will still be taught.

Bibliography

Anderson, Charles W. *Prescribing the Life of the Mind: An Essay on the Purposes of the University, the Aims of Liberal Education, the Competence of Citizens, and the Cultivation of Practical Reason.* Madison: University of Wisconsin Press, 1993.

Barzun, Jacques. *The American University: How It Runs, Where It Is Going,* 2d edition Chicago: University of Chicago Press, 1993.

Bloom, Allan. *The Closing of the American Mind: How Higher Education Has Failed Democracy and Impoverished the Souls of Today's Students.* New York: Simon and Schuster, 1987.

Cole, Jonathan R., Elinor Barber, and Stephen R. Graubard, eds. *The Research University in a Time of Discontent.* Baltimore: Johns Hopkins University Press, 1994.

Cronon, E. David, and John W. Jenkins. *The University of Wisconsin: A History,* vol. 2, 1925–1945. Madison: University of Wisconsin Press, 1994.

Curti, Merle, and Vernon Carstensen. *The University of Wisconsin: A History,* vol. 1, 1848–1925. Madison: University of Wisconsin Press, 1949.

Damrosch, David. *We Scholars: Changing the Culture of the University.* Cambridge: Harvard University Press, 1995.

Hansen, W. Lee, ed. *Academic Freedom on Trial: 100 Years of Sifting and Winnowing at the University of Wisconsin.* Madison: University of Wisconsin, 1998.

Ingraham, Mark H. *From a Wisconsin Soapbox.* Madison: Wisconsin Academy, 1979.

Kimball, Bruce A. *Orators and Philosophers: A History of the Idea of Liberal Education,* expanded edition. New York: College Board, 1955.

Kliebard, Herbert M. *Forging the American Curriculum: Essays in Curriculum History and Theory.* New York: Rutledge, 1992.

Levine, Lawrence W. *The Opening of the American Mind: Canons, Culture, and History.* Boston: Beacon Press, 1996.

Menand, Louis, ed. *The Future of Academic Freedom.* Chicago: University of Chicago Press, 1996.

Nussbaum, Martha C. *Cultivating Humanity : A Classical Defense of Reform in Liberal Education.* Cambridge: Harvard University Press, 1997.

Rosovsky, Henry. *The University: An Owner's Manual.* New York: W. W. Norton, 1991.

Thwaites, Reuben Gold, ed. *The University of Wisconsin: Its History and Its Alumni, with Historical and Descriptive Sketches of Madison.* Madison: J.N. Purcell, 1900.

Using Technology Wisely

NEW APPROACHES TO TEACHING AND LEARNING THROUGH TECHNOLOGY

Kathleen Christoph

TECHNOLOGY PROMPTS US to think about why we teach and learn the way we do, and how we might teach and learn differently using technology. As Chancellor David Ward stated in "A Vision for the Future," "Information technology is a powerful tool. In order to harness this power, we must rethink our traditional approaches to teaching, learning and conducting research."

The power of technology is not speed, flashy colors, or sounds. It is the ability to remove such barriers as class meeting sites, class meeting times, library hours, the traditional semester schedule, even access to a university education.

The extent to which we've embraced these tools is evident in the following statistics, gathered from Division of Information Technology (DoIT) Computing Surveys. In 1998, 98% of University of Wisconsin–Madison students used a computer for academic work. The top three software applications used were word processors (93%), electronic mail or "email" (93%), and Internet browsers (88%). Virtually every student spent some time connected to the Internet, and the most popular area for training among students was web page development.

Looking back to 1992, the top three software applications used by students were word processors (88%), spreadsheets (31%), and programming languages (24%). Only 20 percent of

Kathleen Christoph is director of Learning Technology and Distance Education, Division of Information Technology, and assistant provost for Instructional Technology at the University of Wisconsin–Madison.

students used a modem, and training for email was in the highest demand. There was no World Wide Web.

We assume that students today will have access to computers, will communicate electronically, and will be adept in the use of basic technology tools such as word processors, spreadsheets, and World Wide Web browsers. We take for granted ready access to the Internet from classroom, dormitory, work, or home. We look forward to Internet2 and its increased capacity compared to the "old" Internet. The question is not whether we have the technology, but how we will use it next.

As with any innovation, adoption of technology takes time. First, we learn to use the technology itself, evidenced by the widespread computer use by students, faculty, and staff. Then, we begin to substitute or "bolt on" the new technology to existing instructional activities like lecture materials and handouts. Next, we develop new approaches to teaching and learning that take advantage of the technology. Finally, we discover entirely new uses for the technology. It is only then that we fully realize its impact on teaching and learning and see the potential of using technology wisely.

In the first part of this chapter, I will describe four uses of technology to illustrate how the University of Wisconsin–Madison is adopting technology in teaching and learning. Then, I will highlight how these changes present us with challenges in the areas of faculty and instructional staff support, rewards, intellectual property ownership, and the higher education marketplace. Finally, I will discuss UW–Madison's responses and directions.

How Technology is Used in Teaching and Learning

Instructional technology has become an integral part of the academic experience. Ben Schneiderman, professor at the University of Maryland, likens educational technologies to transportation.

In an article for *Educom Review*, he wrote, "Videoconferencing and electronic classrooms are the supersonic Concordes of our profession; they are expensive and take planning to use, but can do some amazing things. By contrast, listservs and bulletin boards are the buses and trains; they require modest resources and planning, but have a wider impact on daily life. Web access and e-mail are the automobiles; they are widely available and highly flexible to serve individual learner and team needs." All of these technologies lead to new ways of teaching and learning both in and outside the classroom.

Communication among Students and Instructors

Technology facilitates communication between students and instructors and between groups of students both on and off campus. Frequent student-faculty contact in and out of class is an important factor in student motivation and involvement. Faculty concern helps students to get through rough times and to keep on working (Chickering and Gamson, 1987).

Email is a fairly simple technology that yields far-reaching changes. It can improve classroom mechanics and expand office hours. Students who would normally not bother to tell the instructor about a problem with the placement of a projector or the lighting in a classroom can send an email message suggesting a change. Instructors can save class time responding to common questions and making announcements via email. Email offers a way for students to ask questions and bring up concerns that formerly were handled during office hours. Instructors report a dramatic increase in student contacts via email compared to contact via traditional office hours.

Email is not simply convenient; it can facilitate learning through on-line discussions. An electronic classlist, a special listserv containing email addresses of all class members, helps to get these exchanges started. An email exchange before a class meeting can prime a discussion; or, following class it can also be used to continue a discussion. Many students, in particular quiet students, participate in discussions more readily via email. Email allows participants the time to compose or reflect on a question or response. It is a convenient means of communication; both students and faculty can work at their own time, night or day. While email will never completely replace face-to-face communication, it does allow for some communication to take place another way, freeing class time for better use.

Electronic communication facilitates collaboration among students. It introduces learning that is cooperative and social, rather than competitive and isolated. Students who work with others often experience a greater sense of involvement in the learning process. Sharing ideas and responding to others students' ideas improves thinking and deepens understanding (Chickering and Gamson, 1987). A frequent complaint from employers is that graduates often lack the experience and ability to learn collaboratively and work in teams. Students are increasingly gaining this experience through electronic collaboration, without regard for place or time. Students working in groups solve problems via videoconferencing or computer conferencing. Videoconferencing allows individuals to see, hear, and interact with one another over a distance at an established time. Computer conferencing typically involves communication via text and graphics. Each individual chooses when to participate via computer.

In a neurophysiology class at UW–Madison, students were challenged by real medical problems using technology similar to the type they will use in the "real world." Using computer conferencing, the class of 120 students worked in groups of eight students, with each group trying to solve a different medical problem relating to the ear. Drs. John Brugge and Tom Pasic played the role of the "experts on call" and also monitored the communications electronically. The students called on the doctors for their expertise, and the doctors proactively guided those groups in need of help. Each doctor was able to actively participate in multiple groups, something they would not have been able to do effectively in a traditional classroom where all the groups would meet at once. Students were able to problem-solve collaboratively with each other in small groups on their own time.

In another case, four Big Ten institutions offer a wider variety of courses than any one institution could by combining enrollments and rotating the teaching among faculty for a series of political science seminars. Students at the four institutions meet via videoconferencing to participate in seminars such as the one on advanced statistical methods using maximum likelihood estimation. The students view materials, listen to oral information, ask questions, and carry on discussions, much like in a traditional seminar. The main difference is that the other students are in Ohio, Minnesota, and Illinois. Enrollments for these courses at each of the schools would be too low to normally allow offering such specialized seminars. Also, the faculty members at each of the institutions specialize in a different area of advanced data analysis and modeling. By combining enrollments and sharing teaching via technology, both the students and faculty are exposed to a wider variety of topics than otherwise possible.

With students taking classes from different institutions, from work, and from home, communication technologies can bridge distances and help create virtual learning communities. Students experience another way to get to know faculty members and one another. Contrary to instinct, students in classes taught exclusively or nearly exclusively via electronic communications technology often feel more connected to other students than in traditional class settings. One student, reflecting on her relations with her fellow students in an on-line class, said, "I knew them a lot better than in any other classes I've ever taken face to face." This kind of connection is also notable in large classes where there has been little expectation for communication among students or with faculty. Through electronic technology, students and faculty communicate more frequently and more reflectively; a greater sense of community develops. The literature is full of stories of shy students and students from different cultures opening up in and out of class when communications technologies were employed. With the new media, participation and contribution from diverse students become more equitable and widespread (Chickering and Ehrmann, 1997).

Communications technology also has the potential to vastly increase access to education. Since not all students and faculty need to be in the same place, the barriers of distance are gone. New choices exist about the time for instruction and for discussion. With fewer constraints on location and time of classes, more working adults with families are finding a way to participate in higher education. Alumni can also remain active in lifelong learning opportunities made possible through electronic communications technology.

At the University of Wisconsin–Madison, we have an array of communications technologies at our disposal. Students, faculty, and staff are becoming facile in using the new tools for improving existing activities: class logistics, office hours, class discussions, extending access to classes. We are beginning to use the technology in new ways, such as for group problem-solving sessions. Our personal challenges are to learn how to use the appropriate technology for communication (remembering face-to-face has its place); to mix the new communications technologies with the traditional means of communications (email should coexist with letters and phone calls); to integrate innovation with a healthy lifestyle (it can seem as if there is no longer an end to the work day or the class day); in short to use communications technology wisely.

Access to Learning Materials

Just as communication among students and faculty is no longer limited by time and place, more and more learning materials are available any time of the day or night at any location. Technology enables students and faculty to gain access to learning materials quickly and in a variety of media, often delivered via the World Wide Web over the Internet.

Library materials are no longer confined to library buildings.

On-line catalogs help us find traditional materials—books and journals. The CIC Virtual Electronic Library, a consortium of eleven libraries in the Big Ten plus the University of Chicago, is now the largest library in the world outside the Library of Congress through its virtual catalog. Students, faculty, and staff at any of the CIC institutions have access to materials from any of the libraries. Digital materials are available on-line at any time, while traditional materials are shipped via courier. One student commented, "The biggest benefit for me is the time factor. I can do research anytime of the day or night. It's not replacing what I can do in a library, but it does help me narrow down what it is I need to find." For the first time, as of fiscal year 1997, the number of uses of library electronic information resources exceeded the use of library materials in paper format at the University of Wisconsin–Madison. The library provides the materials we want wherever we are, removing time and place barriers to information.

Just as libraries are no longer confined to buildings, course materials and exercises are not confined to classrooms. Ready access to technology-delivered learning materials frees class meeting time for new activities. When Professor John Moore at UW–Madison wanted to make the introductory chemistry laboratory sessions more inquiry-based and open-ended to illustrate the scientific method, the teaching assistants said they would need more lab time. To achieve this, they use technology to free lab time previously spent answering mundane questions about lab techniques. Now, thousands of chemistry students per year use web-based multimedia materials to learn and review lab techniques and to take self-tests prior to coming to class and refer to during class. More lab time is devoted to data gathering, data analysis, hypothesis formation, and hypothesis testing. The instructor's time is freed to guide students to discover for themselves, to work like real-world scientists.

Students in Professor Nick Cahill's Survey of Art History class used to spend much of their discussion section time reviewing slides and other materials presented in lecture. Now, with the images and annotations available via the World Wide Web, students can review material and pursue other information outside of class at their leisure. This frees class time to probe into specific art history issues and, according to Professor Cahill, "to actually hold discussions in the discussion session."

Not only does technology allow easier access to materials, it provides instructors new ways to customize course materials. Digital media can be easily broken into bits and pieces and put together in any way imaginable. Materials are not confined in a container such as a book, nor are they constrained to linear presentation. Professor Cahill says, "You can recombine things in new ways that wouldn't be serviced by traditional text books. The ability to put something together yourself from pieces is a really important one. It makes it possible to turn your focus to new things that you wouldn't otherwise be able to do."

Learning materials are more accessible and customizable, and they are also richer. Digital media can be dynamic and up-to-date and contain graphics, animation, video, and audio. They can easily and immediately link to related information world-wide. Instructors can mix and match a variety of media for courses.

Professor Joan Wildman's web site for her jazz improvisation course offers text, graphics, music notation, and audio via the World Wide Web. Previously she was confined to offering students audio tapes or individual instruction on jazz motives (organized series of pitches/rhythms consisting of only a few notes). Now students go to the web site to see, listen to, replay, and practice the motives at their convenience. Professor Wildman also offers multiple links on her web site to historical and related resources, so students can easily explore an area of interest in depth by following the links. Professor Wildman's time is freed from presenting the same content over and over to guiding the students in their learning and their interests.

Technology offers students a staggering amount of options to learn by doing. Professor Steve Ackerman uses the World Wide

Web to offer exercises to students in his Introduction to Weather and Climate class. Realizing the power of animation and interactions in weather and the fact students learn better by doing, Professor Ackerman moved from simply presenting learning materials to thinking about the active learning potential of the web and how to get students involved. Now, he offers sophisticated interactive exercises in decoding surface weather plots and in contouring for students to actually learn and practice the skills on-line. Students can take as much time as they need to cover the concepts, and they can practice until they understand the material.

Another advantage of on-line materials is the ability to easily share materials across disciplines. Professor Bill Berg uses art history images with students in his French Language and Culture class. He simply links to selected images from his class web page. Professor Moore encourages advanced biology and engineering classes to use chemistry materials for review and reference. This demonstrates how on-line resources have the potential to make courses more interdisciplinary by making materials more easily accessible.

With ready access to learning materials, students can take the time saved on acquiring materials to devote to sharpening their cognitive skills of analysis, synthesis, application, and evaluation. The faculty role can take the time saved on delivering materials to move from "sage on the stage" to "guide on the side," helping students discern what is worth studying and helping them develop deeper understanding and beliefs. Students develop skills in higher-order thinking and can move away from strict memorization of facts.

At the University of Wisconsin–Madison, we have ready access to computers and networks to deliver learning materials. Students, faculty, and staff are growing accustomed to accessing library materials on-line. Students expect to receive course syllabi, announcements, notes, and materials on-line, and faculty are finding this convenient and useful. We are beginning to discover new applications for teaching and learning via the World Wide

Web as demonstrated by the weather exercises and the examples of sharing resources among disciplines described above. Our challenge is to keep experimenting with new ways to access new types of learning materials, constantly evaluating their merit, keeping what works, and using traditional means where appropriate. In these ways, we will wisely employ technology for access to learning materials.

New Tools for Teaching and Learning

The sections above have outlined how communications technology allows increased contact between faculty and students and among students, and how it provides ways for students to collaborate either on campus or at a distance. Technology also gives easier access to a wider variety of learning materials. Exciting new developments in visual, audio, and interactive technologies offer many opportunities for new ways of teaching and learning.

Multimedia

Multimedia offers the opportunity to convey concepts in a way not possible with traditional teaching tools. Not only can we convey concepts more effectively, we can convey ideas that seemed prohibitively difficult to express in the past.

Students in Pam Scheibel's nursing class learn about the anatomy of the respiratory system and the physiology of breathing through an interactive multimedia CD-ROM. They see the lungs move and hear the breathing. They learn to compare normal function to abnormal, by listening, as in real life, and by seeing the lungs through animation. Dr. Scheibel says, "I think technology, especially visual, really helps students understand the concepts rather than me just saying it and them thinking about it. It doesn't replace the teacher. It's just such a wonderful adjunct."

In Dr. Nancy Rasmussen's elementary education music class, students learn about music without having to know standard music notation. Her students are not trained musicians and do not read or write music. Dr. Rasmussen uses computer animation synchronized to music to help students understand what they hear. Says one student, "It made it a lot easier. She explains the rhythms and beats over the computer. It clicked." Through multimedia technology, visual learners can understand concepts without needing special skills or being able to turn text or symbols into images in their heads.

Simulation

Computers can be used to simulate real-life situations. Simulations offer students a chance to develop and practice skills not otherwise possible or practical in the classroom.

When faced with a budget cut, instructors in a genetics class turned to the computer to take over the breeding of fruit flies. A commercial software package was programmed to generate the fruit flies according to a scientifically accurate model. The students organize the data and analyze the results. The software allows students to do more experiments breeding more flies than in the past. They can also breed rabbits, butterflies, or custom-programmed species, and the computer helps students analyze the results more quickly.

Students on campus and in industry play the role of manager in Professor Randall Dunham's management simulation on motivation. The multimedia CD-ROM-based program places the student in an office with all the normal tools at hand: a desk, a telephone, personnel files, and reference books. In addition, it offers multimedia tutorials, case studies, and self-assessments. The student manages as many as five employees, making decisions and facing outcomes based on those decisions. Through this simulated management experience, the student discovers and comes to understand many of the theories of motivation. It is unlikely that a college student would be able to actually manage five employees as a class assignment. Professor Dunham's simulation makes this possible providing the prompting and feedback necessary to guide the students through the process and to learn about motivation.

Individualized Learning

Technology can provide individual students with the practice, interaction, and assessment necessary to learn certain skills. It can even out the varying skills of students before entering a class and provide review for concepts not understood in class. By combining individual assessment with self-paced study, technology can help reduce the frustration of students ahead of or behind the level of the class.

When a new undergraduate general education requirement on communications was instituted, the library created a multimedia tutorial to help 5,400 students learn and practice the basic library skills and strategies that were a part of the requirement. Through simulated database searches, students on the CD-ROM teach the students taking the tutorial. Students are allowed to practice skills and take self-tests as many times as they wish. By allowing students to spend as much time as they like on various modules and by providing interactive exercises, the tutorial accommodates students' varied levels of experience in using libraries and ensures that all students can gain the basic library skills needed to use the vast resources available in campus libraries.

The allowance computers can make for individual differences can improve comprehension and enhance learning. Students practice reading difficult Hebrew texts on their own time and at their own pace with Professor Gilead Morahg's Hebrew Helper program. Hebrew Helper provides extensive assistance, prompting, and resources to students. Professor Morahg finds the students' comprehension of the text has increased since introducing the program, and the students have greater confidence in their understanding of the text. He says, "Students can work their level of competence up to where they want to be. This we can't provide in a classroom or through homework." He also observes that it is a great equalizer and that "The interactive dimension of computer assisted learning, if correctly designed, really stimulates the students. They actually spend more focused time working with this, and enjoy it more, because of constant reinforcement."

Among the powerful uses of technology, developing new teaching and learning tools is often the most time-consuming and costly. A complex simulation or tutorial can take more than a year to develop. On the other hand, a simple animation to accompany a lecture can be quite reasonable.

At the University of Wisconsin–Madison, instructors are using animation and multimedia in lectures to illustrate dynamic processes and to convey complex content. Students are using simulations to gain real-life experiences not possible in the classroom or laboratory and tutorials to practice skills. We must make wise decisions on when and how to employ these new tools for teaching and learning. The key is to clearly identify an instructional problem and to accurately assess whether technology can solve the problem and at what cost. Our instructional problems remain fairly stable, while the availability, ease of use, and cost of the technology tools improve. This amounts to a moving target of a vast array of new tools for teaching and learning, and we are thus challenged to use them wisely.

Restructuring Courses and Programs

Identifying appropriate technology tools to address our instructional problems is a definite challenge. Drastically changing the structure of our courses and programs prompted by the availability of technology is yet another dimension of change.

It is typical for faculty and instructional staff to begin using technology as a substitute for existing instructional methods. A case in point is the use of presentation technology to present bulleted speaking points in place of the overhead transparency or chalkboard. Carol Twigg of Educom terms this "bolt on" use of technology. This should not be construed as negative. It is the beginning of a process. Though "bolt on" use of technology may not evoke a learning revolution, it does offer instructors a way to "try on" technology for teaching, to observe its potential impact on students, and to become comfortable with technology. It is not until faculty reach a comfort level with technology and are convinced that it will have a positive effect on student learning that they are willing to invest the time and energy to engage in genuine pedagogical innovation.

Our adoption of information technology for teaching and learning at UW–Madison is following the three stages outlined by Bill Massy in "The Learning Revolution":

1. Productivity aids, which allow faculty and students to do familiar things faster and more effectively like word processing, spreadsheets and electronic mail.
2. Enrichment add-ons, which introduce new materials into the curriculum without changing the basic mode of instruction, such as access to materials via the Web and use of multimedia presentations and simulations
3. Stimulants and enablers of educational process reengineering, in which the educational process is redesigned to optimize the use of technology to better serve the student (Massy, 1996).

The first and second stages enhance educational quality, but they do not change the basic instructional paradigm. They do not add up to a learning revolution. Examples of the third stage, characterized by real paradigm shifts, are beginning to emerge.

Two introductory chemistry courses, which enroll 4,400 students per year at the University of Wisconsin–Madison, are being reconfigured by Professor John Moore to include more individualized learning opportunities for students and fewer lecture and face-to-face discussion hours. The initial ideas and developments were seeded by a grant from the National Science Foundation called "Establishing New Traditions: Revitalizing the Chemistry Curriculum," which included a coalition of colleges, universities, and two-year colleges. A major challenge in introductory chemistry is working with students coming from a variety of backgrounds. Some have a strong pre-college experience from excellent high schools; others have inadequate chemistry background; some enter with no background. At present, it is difficult to deal with this broad range of student preparation, because little individualization of instruction is possible. The new approach will change this by employing on-line, interactive, modular tutorials and assessment. In addition to individualizing the instruction, the technology-based materials will also allow students to review chemistry in subsequent courses and will include examples and information from other disciplines that will help students to see the applications of the chemistry they are learning. To accomplish this change requires the professor to shift from a transmitter of knowledge via lecture to designer of individualized interactive materials and guide for the students. Teaching assistants will spend less time in lecture and discussion and will move to developing and assessing the interactive modules and to guiding individual students. Students will be less passive and more engaged in learning through individualized materials and will receive more guidance for solving individual problems.

Another example of significant change is a new interdisciplinary, graduate-level certificate in quality improvement being pioneered by Professor Mark Finster of the School of Business. This program is designed to increase access to nationally recognized faculty in the area of quality improvement. Currently, the courses that will form the basis for the certificate are taught in a classroom using interactive case studies. Only a few students can take such a faculty-intensive class at any one time. Also, since many potential students are working, it can be difficult to come to Madison or to attend at the time the courses are offered. Through web-based technology, more students will be able to take the courses and work at their own location and time. They will learn content in small modules and receive individualized feedback and direction. As active participants in an on-line learning community, they will work in virtual teams on projects relevant to their interests and their careers. Through technology and innovative program design, more students coming from a wide variety of backgrounds will have access to education in quality improvement.

The changes being undertaken in introductory chemistry and

in quality improvement courses are truly educational reengineering endeavors. A common characteristic of the two is that they are adapted to students with a variety of backgrounds and a range of personal and professional goals. The resulting redesigned courses will provide an evolutionary pathway leading from the current synchronous attendance model of instruction to an asynchronous distributed model. In the new model, each student's background, current pedagogical needs, and future aspirations regarding course of study and vocation will be used to create a unique experience for the student.

Professor Schneiderman, continuing his analogy of educational technologies as transportation says, "So the truly technology-entranced professor who wants to fly has signed up for pilot training. But the rest of us can manifest the right stuff by getting our students to be effective users of the commonly available information technologies. However, the goal is successful learning—not merely to get students to use these technologies. We are not out to promote bus riding or car cruising. The courageous professor has a pedagogic or curricular destination in mind and knows that the technology is just the vehicle for getting there."

The Challenge of Change

Designing a course is still about choosing destinations and how to get there. No one technology is a panacea, nor is technology in itself a solution. To use technology wisely, change is required of individuals (faculty, staff, and students) and of our institutions. Beyond the challenges of selecting and using technology, we face additional challenges of training and supporting faculty and instructional staff, rewarding teaching and learning, clarifying ownership of intellectual property, and responding to competition among institutions in the new educational marketplace.

Training and Supporting Faculty and Instructional Staff
Faculty and instructional staff need to reach a comfort level with

technology and need to be convinced that it will have a positive effect on student learning before they are willing to invest the time and energy to engage in genuine teaching innovation. This is a big step, and it requires support from the institution. This step is crucial if we are to experience the transformational power of technology.

Adoption of technology for teaching by faculty and instructional staff closely follows the pattern described by William H. Geoghegan in his article, "What Ever Happened to Instructional Technology?", which elaborates on the ideas in the work of E. M. Rogers and G. A. Moore. Some faculty, around 10 to 15 percent, are excited by the technology itself. They typically learn about new technology with little assistance, and they experiment on their own to see how new technologies might influence their teaching. They are the "innovators" and "early adopters." They are risk-takers, accustomed to occasional failure. Individuals in these groups work independently and look for occasional technical help.

This is the group that creates the early examples of how new technologies can change teaching and learning. They are generally enthusiastic about sharing their findings and experiences with other early adopters and with the larger faculty audience. Communicating their results and excitement to their colleagues through seminars, articles, and meetings helps raise overall faculty awareness of the potential of technology in teaching and learning.

A much larger group of faculty, the "early majority" comprises the next 35 to 40 percent. These faculty members are not excited by the technology itself but are interested in using technology only if they can clearly see the benefits technology can bring to teaching and learning. This group says, "Convince me that technology will help," followed by "What will work best for me?" and "Who will help me do it?" They focus on pedagogy. They are not interested in experimenting with technology just because it is new and may hold some promise.

This group responds well to solid examples of successes by their respected colleagues to gain awareness of the benefits. In contrast to their "early adopter" colleagues, these faculty members do not wish to implement technological change on their own. They look for and evaluate successful examples. They ask for help in deciding what will work best for them and in creating new materials or restructuring parts of a course to incorporate technology. They tend to pay close attention to their time. They choose to learn to use new technologies once they perceive that the time investment is reasonable compared to the benefits. If it is not, they turn to staff or students to do it for them or decide to hold off. Any training must be targeted specifically to their individual needs.

Here lies an economic challenge for the university: how to find faculty time and assistance. One answer is faculty release time. This option is costly and is not widely used at the University of Wisconsin–Madison. Another is staff assistance. We are seeing definite shifts in the jobs of departmental support staff to include working with technology in ways that contribute to the creation of technology-based instructional materials or help support technology-mediated courses. College and school technology support staff are moving from technical support to instructional support. The central technology organization supports faculty and instructional staff through a unit dedicated to learning technology.

The technology support is not adequate enough to provide individual assistance for all interested faculty and instructional staff. Recently some help has come from UW System and from internal reallocations. Programs to train and enlist the help of students are being created. On-line and "just in time" training is growing. Grant programs such as the Hilldale Foundation Supported Instructional Technology Grants, the College of Letters and Science IN-TIME grants, the School of Business Eagles program, and the Division of Information Technology Web Grants Program provide some relief.

The bright side is that while the amount of support in both personnel and money is rising modestly, the technology is also becoming easier to use and more widely accepted. Few people would be willing to give up their word processor or spreadsheet at this point. Some instructional technologies are close to reaching this level of use and acceptance as an everyday tool; classroom presentation technology and electronic mail are examples of this.

As we move into this stage, the next 40 percent of faculty and instructional staff, the "late majority," will join. Members of this group are hesitant to learn the technologies. They typically wait until the technology is a given and can see the benefits well established before they adopt the technology. This group has generally accepted word processing but is not yet involved with instructional technologies. The final 10 to 15 percent, the "laggards," may never show an interest.

It is not likely that the University of Wisconsin–Madison will provide significantly more faculty release time or vastly increase its instructional support personnel in the near future. We do know, however, the roles of support personnel will change and technology will become easier to use. In order to make wise use of technology and avoid wasting our precious few resources, we must train faculty in technology skills when the time investment is reasonable, provide direct help when specialized technical skills are required, and constantly direct the use of technology in ways that will fully demonstrate its impact on teaching and learning.

Trent Batson and Judy Williamson sum up the need for faculty training and support: "The individual and departmental transition process is coordinated with the institution-wide process of transition around technology . . . In a time of revolutionary change in the knowledge-making processes in our culture, faculty development must itself take on a new role, not of helping faculty improve their performance in the status quo, but of empowering them to re-create a new order" (Batson and Williamson).

Rewards

As there is a need for faculty development, there is also a need for rewarding individuals for wise use of technology in teaching. Batson and Williamson say, "Individual faculty members cannot be expected, on their own, to go off quixotically tilting at the windmills of the established order on campus, assuming the entire risk of revolutionary change in their teaching approach, and with no reward or compensation" (Batson and Williamson).

Rewards are needed in two areas, one for the development of quality technology-based learning materials and the other for the improvement of teaching and learning using existing technologies.

The university has the talent and resources to be a primary source for development of high-quality, widely distributed, technology-based learning materials. Recognition should be given to development projects that contribute to the quality of technology-based instruction in the field. To encourage this, such development should be acknowledged as an important part of the university's mission and rewarded accordingly. For the most part, this is not the case now. When Professor Gilead Morahg advises his colleagues about technology development, he advises caution and is pessimistic about the future of development if the present situation persists: "Without proper support and incentive, think long and hard before getting involved. Demands of time are very great. The struggle for funds is constant. And there is a sad lack of academic recognition for such projects. As long as the development of computer-assisted instructional materials for general use is not given credit similar to that of research, I doubt that we will be able to utilize the great potential of instructional technology in a systematic way." A recognition that the development of outstanding technology-based learning materials is, in some cases, equally valuable as research for purposes of promotion and merit compensation would encourage faculty and staff to work toward creating new technology.

Adopting and using existing technology-based materials to improve the learning environment for students is also an area that should be encouraged through recognition and reward. Just as not every faculty member is expected to write a textbook, it is not reasonable to expect everyone to develop technology-based learning materials. Nor is it practical. However, as more quality technology-based materials are developed, effectively using them to improve teaching and learning will continue to be a challenge. As described earlier, technology opens new possibilities for improving students' understanding of complex concepts, for individualizing instruction, and even for offering courses and programs to new audiences at their place and time. The institution should encourage its members to constantly seek ways to improve student learning through technology enhancements to a course, restructuring courses to incorporate technology, and creation of new academic programs. Recognition for successful efforts should be incorporated into the existing and evolving channels for rewarding teaching excellence.

Rewards for the creation of technology-based learning materials and for their use in improving teaching and learning are necessary to achieve widespread wise use of technology.

Intellectual Property

While rewards for creation and use of technology in teaching are challenging, so are the issues relating to ownership and control of the technology-based materials and courses.

Nationally, issues of intellectual property are some of the hottest. A recent article in the *Chronicle of Higher Education* stated, "For centuries, professors have prepared lectures, organized readings, and created exams without worrying about who owned them. But now the growth of distance education and the widespread use of multimedia course materials have convinced some administrators and faculty members that they're sitting on gold mines: It might be possible to package college courses and sell them over the Internet or on disks."

It is the practice at the University of Wisconsin–Madison for faculty and instructional staff to own their intellectual property, the legal rights to the products of their ideas. Faculty and instructional staff have always created syllabi, reading lists, and handouts for courses. The university claims no rights to these, nor to textbooks or articles. On the other hand, policies and processes have been established for the sharing of income from licenses for inventions.

Where do digital instructional materials or courses fit? Are they like textbooks, like inventions, or neither?

It is common for faculty to contract directly with publishers to create textbooks and to reap the financial benefits. The faculty provide the content, and the publisher supplies the editors, the graphic arts, the marketing, and the distribution. The university's contribution is minimal. The publisher owns the product. The faculty collect royalties. The university maintains a hands-off position.

The Bayh-Dole Act and university policy determine the process for disclosure and dissemination of inventions. Most inventions are patented and licensed through the Wisconsin Alumni Research Foundation (WARF). There is typically a significant university contribution to the invention through labs, equipment or personnel. Faculty members work through University-Industry Relations (UIR) to assign rights to WARF. The university, department, and the individual (faculty, staff, or student) all share the royalties.

For technology-based instructional materials, it is common for the university to contribute to the development and production (through programmers, instructional designers, computer hardware, and software), although publishers or grants also fund or provide this development. Most materials fall under copyright law, not patent law. Thus far, the university has not closely tracked its contribution nor imposed rules of ownership because of it.

The climate is changing. In 1995 Chancellor Ward commissioned a Technology Transfer Committee, chaired by Professor Lloyd Smith, to make recommendations to improve the University of Wisconsin–Madison technology transfer process. This committee identified seven major issues, one of which involved software copyright. The committee wrote: "There is an unusually high level of uncertainty and ambiguity in the area of

UW policy regarding copyright law and computer software. As the economic impact of this type of intellectual property continues to expand; it is important that the University have in place sound and well-reasoned policies."

As a result of this report, a Task Force on Software Intellectual Property was created with representatives from faculty, staff, students, legal services, and technology transfer. The group met for nearly a year and issued a set of recommendations based on a motivation to "make available to faculty, staff, students and the University the privileges, rewards, and responsibilities associated with the creation of copyrightable software intellectual property" and to find a "clear way to interact with the private sector to develop the financial rewards of copyrightable works, particularly software." It recommended keeping current policies but clarifying them and improving the processes that are used to implement the policies.

The University of Wisconsin–Madison does not generally claim ownership rights to copyrighted materials. To change this would mean a major policy decision and a dramatic change in climate. There is disagreement on whether there is a need for a change in policy and practice. However, there is widespread agreement that there is a need for a policy as well as for awareness and guidance on ownership of intellectual property. As Graham B. Spanier, president of Pennsylvania State University recently said, "To have no policy will most likely cause major dysfunction in the years ahead." The challenge is to encourage the creation and dissemination of knowledge while acting fiscally and ethically responsible as a public entity.

The New Educational Marketplace

As knotty as the issues of intellectual property might be, technology is also prompting changes in higher education spanning far-reaching areas. Because student populations entering higher education represent a range of ages and experiences, many more institutions, and a wider variety of institutions, are evolving. As technology expands the opportunities for teaching and learning, so it also opens new markets in higher education and creates competition.

Technology lowers the threshold for entry into the higher education provider marketplace. Ted Marchese, in an article for the *AAHE Bulletin*, talks about competition in terms of the convenience market, courses at a distance, and niches. He tells how Wisconsin recently counted more than 100 out-of-state degree providers within its borders, with 37 in Milwaukee alone. The University of Phoenix, whose buildings are seen along busy interstate highways in nearly every major city in the United States, has 48,000 degree-credit students at 111 learning centers in 32 states. Phoenix's phenomenal growth has been largely driven by niche programs at the BA-completion and master's-degree levels, especially in business, information technology, and teacher education. Sylvan Learning Systems (1–800-EDUCATE), a Wall Street darling, aims to be the world's "leading provider of educational services to families, schools, and industry." Marchese says, "In the convenience end of the market, everybody goes after the other guy's lunch."

Other competition comes through institutions offering courses at a distance. Western Governors University, a highly publicized multistate virtual university involving 17 governors and 14 business partners, will not employ teaching faculty, develop courses, or grant credits. Instead it will be a broker of courses and programs. According to Marchese, "Its business plan envisions 95,000 students by early next century . . . Utah governor Mike Leavitt foresees WGU becoming the New York Stock Exchange of technology-delivered courses." Similar undertakings can be seen with the California Virtual University and the Southern Regional Educational Board's Southern Regional Electronic Campus. The National Technological University, a nonprofit of which UW–Madison is a member, has been beaming engineering coursework from 50 major universities to clients worldwide for 14 years (Marchese, 1998).

The CIC (Big Ten plus University of Chicago) is turning competition into cooperation with its new Common Market of Courses and Institutes (CMCI), offering a "mechanism for joint enrollment and reimbursement by which the CIC universities can share with each other knowledge and expertise that is difficult to find and to keep and that cannot practically be maintained by more than a few universities." The CMCI is beginning by sharing specialized courses at the graduate level. UW–Madison students, along with others at several institutions, are taking a course on "Emerging Technologies: Collaboration and Visualization Tools in Society" from the University of Illinois and the National Center for Supercomputing Applications. The CMCI plans to move toward offering whole new programs in the near future.

Some higher education institutions are working directly with industry to fill niches. One of the most visible is the Michigan Virtual Automotive College (MVAC). Our peers the University of Michigan and Michigan State University have joined together with the state of Michigan, the Big Three automakers, and the United Auto Workers to "offer the best courses from any provider anywhere to corporate employees." MVAC's president is former University of Michigan president Jim Duderstadt. The executive committee is chaired by MSU president Peter McPherson. According to Marchese, "The essential idea behind MVAC—that an industry group can combine to produce its own education enterprise, entry-level through lifelong learning, and cease reliance on a 'cottage industry' of existing campuses—has strong appeal among corporate execs, especially where dissatisfaction with traditional higher education is high. In the face of such a combine (and such course quality), observers feel, few colleges could maintain competitive offerings, on campus or off."

While technology elicits competition, so does it open doors to markets. Close to $300 billion is spent each year on postsecondary education and training. In addition, industry already spends $58 billion a year on employee training and development and sees distance technologies as a way to save time and cut costs (by 15% to 50%). To the business-minded, the postsecondary education and training market looms large and appears ripe for the picking . . . an "addressable market opportunity at the dawn of a new paradigm," in the words of Morgan Stanley Dean Witter (Marchese, 1998).

Given the competition and the market, it is not at all surprising that state policymakers' enthusiasm for the application of information technology to higher education is at an all-time high according to James R. Mingle, Executive Director, State Higher Education Executive Officers (Heterick, Mingle, Twigg, 1998). Wisconsin is no exception.

Responses and Directions

The University of Wisconsin–Madison is in an enviable position to take advantage of advances in technology. It has strong partnerships statewide, regionally, and nationally. The state of Wisconsin, with its BadgerNet and instructional technology initiatives, is making great strides in building a robust technology infrastructure and in sharing academic programs among its 26 University of Wisconsin campuses. UW–Madison has been collaborating with peer institutions in the CIC for over 40 years. The new CIC Common Market of Courses and Institutes is, as stated in its promotional brochure, "moving CIC universities one step closer to making *all* of the instructional potential of *all* of its universities available to *all* of its students." Nationally, UW–Madison is an active participant in many initiatives including the Educause National Learning Infrastructure Initiative (NLII), which identifies key issues facing higher education in transforming education through information technology and developing leadership to address those issues.

Through its partnerships, and by using its intellectual and financial resources wisely, UW–Madison is making incremental, thoughtful, and solid advances in using appropriate technologies to improve teaching and learning. It realizes that technology is not likely to create a learning revolution anytime soon. At the same time, technology can help us pace learning to students' needs and abilities, allow instructors to be more of a "guide on the side" rather than a "sage on the stage," involve students in active and collaborative learning, and provide access to instruction with fewer barriers of time and place, as evidenced by the numerous examples of how UW–Madison faculty and instructional staff are making this happen.

UW–Madison is taking a very practical view of technology by focusing on technology as supportive of our teaching mission and institutional strategy, rather than seeing technology as driving mission or strategy. This allows us to focus on learning, and to look at the debate on traditional residential learning and distance learning in a useful way. Chris Dede talks about "a transformation of conventional distance education—which replicates traditional classroom teaching across barriers of distance and time—into an alternative instructional paradigm: distributed learning." New term or not, it should be clear that, as Dede says, "distributed learning experiences will be seen as vital for all learners even when the same content could be taught face-to-face, and all teaching will have some attributes of distance education" (Dede, 1997). There will be no distinct line between residential learning and distance learning. UW–Madison has long recognized this and looks at how technology can enhance its traditional programs, open access to new students, and create opportunities for new programs.

The university is responding to the challenge of new markets and new opportunities for distributed learning by identifying its niche and targeting areas ripe for transformation. As Chancellor Ward observes, "We have already begun to see a decrease in the number of students in formal postgraduate education in some disciplines. Students are moving quickly into the work sector after a bachelor's degree but often require different kinds of continuing professional education" (Ward, 1997). The chancellor has responded by funding a new program of capstone experiences, certificates, and master's degrees targeting postbaccalaureate education. Through the new programs, professionals in fields as diverse as geography, landscape architecture, and political science will learn skills in geographic information systems. Business students wishing to work in France or with French companies will learn about French language, culture, and business practices. Students in social sciences will gain valuable skills in the computational sciences.

The UW–Madison College of Engineering is responding to the demand for professional education with its new Master's of Engineering in Professional Practice. It is designed to be taught at a distance to working professionals who want to advance their careers without interrupting them. The curriculum, described as an engineer's version of an MBA, focuses on technical and organizational skills critical to modern engineers. The engineering program is following a successful UW–Madison model in administrative medicine, which has offered a technology-mediated advanced degree for years. Both are examples of how UW–Madison is taking advantage of new opportunities afforded by technology to target a niche in the educational marketplace aligned with institutional strategy.

New technologies bring challenges to our traditions, our assumptions, our support structures, and our market. Yet, far from forcing us away from our mission, wise use of technology allows us to express a continuing commitment to learning in new and exciting ways. Through technology, the undergraduate student can experience more individualized instruction and be more connected to other students. The graduate student can participate in seminars with students and faculty from peer institutions. The working adult can join the learning community through distance learning. Each type of student benefits from the new approaches to teaching and learning through technology.

As Chancellor David Ward stated in "A Vision for the Future," "New technologies give us the opportunity to rethink the instructional role of faculty and staff and to redefine student learning." UW–Madison is assessing its existing strengths, expertise, and traditions, and is matching these to the new opportunities afforded by technology to transform teaching and learning and to use technology wisely.

Bibliography

Batson, Trent, and Judy Williamson. *STEPS: A Strategy for Technologically Enlightened Pedagogies (A Work In Progress)*. A Program for Faculty Development Sponsored Collaboratively by The Epiphany Project and The Teaching, Learning, and Technology Roundtables Program of The American Association for Higher Education.
(http://mason.gmu.edu/~epiphany/docs/steps.html)

Chickering, Art, and Zelda Gamson. "Seven Principles for Good Practice in Undergraduate Education." *AAHE Bulletin*, March 1987.

Chickering, Arthur W., and Stephen C. Ehrmann. "Implementing the Seven Principles: Technology as Lever."
(http://www.aahe.org/technology/ehrmann.html)

CRE Association of European Universities. *Restructuring the University: New Technologies for Teaching and Learning: Guidance to Universities on Strategy.* CRE Guide no. 1 (April 1998).

Dede, Chris. "From Distance Education to Distributed Learning." *NLII Viewpoint* 2, no. 1 (Fall/Winter 1997).
(http://www.educom.edu/program/nlii/articles/dede.html)

Division of Information Technology, University of Wisconsin–Madison. 1998 and 1992 Student Computing Surveys. (The 1992 survey is not online, but the URL for 98 is http://www.wisc.edu/doit/research/student98.html)

Geoghegan, William H. "What Ever Happened to Instructional Technology?" Paper presented at the 22nd Annual Conference of the International Business Schools Computing Association, Baltimore, Maryland, July 17–20, 1994.
(http://w3.scale.uiuc.edu/scale/links/library/geoghegan/wpi.html)

Guernsey, Lisa, and Jeffrey R. Young. "Who Owns On-Line Courses?" *Chronicle of Higher Education,* June 5, 1998.

Heterick, Robert C. Jr., James R. Mingle, and Carol A. Twigg. *The Public Policy Implications of a Global Learning Infrastructure.* Washington, DC: Educom, 1998. (http://www.educom.edu/program/nlii/keydocs/policy.html)

Marchese, Ted. "Not-So-Distant Competitors: How New Providers Are Remaking the Postsecondary Marketplace." *AAHE Bulletin,* May 1998.

Schneiderman, Ben. "Educational Journeys on the Web Frontier." *Educom Review,* November/December 1998. (http://www.educause.edu/)

Technology and Its Ramifications for Data Systems: Report of the Policy Panel on Technology, cosponsored by the National Postsecondary Education Cooperative and George Washington University, May 1998.

Ward, David. "Instruction and Technology—An Integral Pair." Faculty Toolbox, Spring 1997. (http://www.wisc.edu/doit/news/facultytoolbox/spring97/)

Change and Innovation in Graduate and Professional Education in Major Public Research Universities

THE *FIN DE SIÈCLE* AND BEYOND

Clifton F. Conrad

THE UNIVERSITY OF WISCONSIN–MADISON, along with other such distinguished public research universities as the University of California-Berkeley and the University of Michigan, has been instrumental in making graduate and professional education the "crown jewel" of higher education in this country—not to mention the envy of universities throughout the world. While this heritage unmistakably represents one of academe's greatest strengths, the challenges facing our nation's public research universities on the eve of the millennium invite serious reflection on the present and future of graduate and professional education in public research universities. My intent throughout this chapter is to encourage such reflection.

I begin by sketching two legacies: one, a history of distinction in graduate education of providing high-quality advanced training; the other a history of typically reluctant accommodation to change and innovation. While our legacy of distinction has served us well, I suggest that our tradition of reluctant accommodation is unlikely to do likewise in the twenty-first century. The remainder of the chapter advances a template for change and innovation, one that at once builds on our legacy of distinction while it concurrently calls for the transformation of graduate and professional education.

Clifton F. Conrad is professor of educational administration at the University of Wisconsin–Madison.

Two Legacies: One of Distinction, One of Reluctant Accommodation to Change

Since the doctorate was introduced at Yale University in 1861, and, not long after, at such universities as Harvard and Wisconsin, one of the most distinguishing features of American higher education has been advanced study. Another feature, pioneering research—especially scientific research—has been from the outset closely linked with advanced study. Together they have been skillfully intertwined for more than a century to provide this legacy of distinction: preparing people for careers in *university teaching* and *scientific research* by providing high-quality advanced graduate training—especially at the Ph.D. level—that combines specialized teaching with hands-on research experience. This legacy, arguably the cornerstone of a long tradition of tremendous public and private support for higher education, scarcely requires elaboration.

While the legacy of providing high-quality graduate education is well known, less visible is another legacy long associated with graduate education in public universities: a tradition of reluctant accommodation to change and innovation. To be sure, major public research universities have introduced some significant changes and innovations in graduate and professional education, especially during the last three decades. Most conspicuous has been the relatively recent rise of the master's degree as a bona fide terminal degree—at least as viewed by many employers and program graduates—rather than simply as a steppingstone to the doctorate. Roughly three-fourths of the graduate degrees currently awarded in our nation's public research universities are awarded at the master's level.

The rise of master's education has been accompanied by another major dimension of change and innovation, the "professionalization" of graduate education. In a nutshell, the emergence of professional education as a signature feature of graduate education represents a direct response to market pressures from students and employers who—following the shift from an industrial to a knowledge-based society—have called for new master's and doctoral programs in professional fields that certify students for a range of high-level positions in many different professions. The rapid expansion of professional program offerings at both the master's and doctoral levels has included the introduction of new discipline-based fields such as applied anthropology and applied history and new interdisciplinary fields such as environmental studies and genetic counseling. Today, close to one-half of the Ph.D.'s granted in public research universities are in professional fields of study, and well over four-fifths of master's degrees are in professional fields.

While one can point to these and many other developments, such as the rise of part-time study and the introduction of new instructional technologies, it is also true that most prestigious public research universities have typically incorporated most changes and reforms with skepticism. In effect, they have embraced an attitude of reluctant accommodation to change and innovation while focusing on doctoral education. Tellingly, as we learned in the national study of master's programs that we conducted several years ago (as cited in the references section), the rise of the master's degree—in concert with the rapid growth of professional programs—has been a "silent success" within higher education, especially from the standpoint of many faculty and administrators in major research universities. As we came to understand, master's programs continue to be viewed as ancillary to Ph.D. programs, and professional programs as ancillary to programs in the liberal arts and sciences in research universities. Meanwhile, some of the most promising changes and innovations in graduate and professional education have taken place outside of research universities.

Why, does the continuing legacy of reluctant accommodation to change and innovation persist in public research universities? To begin with, although enrollments at the doctoral level have periodically declined in recent years, doctoral programs—especially during periods of declining enrollment—have been sustained by the continuous growth of master's enrollments, buoyed by strong state and federal support, and helped by economic and technological demands for highly-trained scientists and professionals. Not surprisingly, there has been a strong tendency within academe to embrace a linear model that, by extrapolation, suggests that graduate and professional education will inevitably rebound from any downturns in the foreseeable future. After all, haven't we invariably rebounded from each downturn in the last three decades? Given this pervasive optimism, it is no small wonder that many administrators and faculty at major public universities are hesitant to embrace change and innovation.

Further, many faculty—and some administrators—are not only convinced that change and innovation threaten our historic legacy of distinction, but they have strong vested interests in the status quo. At the risk of heresy, let this be said as gently as possible: For many faculty in research universities, there is considerable personal benefit in maintaining allegiance to Ph.D. programs that not only provide them with a safe haven but also with a steady stream of students who often contribute substantially to their research programs at relatively low cost. Change and innovation that in any way threatens to disturb the close connection between faculty research and advanced graduate training—a link that remains part and parcel of our legacy of distinction—finds no small resistance among many faculty in research universities.

For these reasons, the conventional wisdom in many of our public research universities seems to be that change and innovation should be approached cautiously in the near future. At the least, it should not be allowed to undermine our legacy of distinction, namely, to provide high-quality advanced graduate training—especially at the Ph.D. level in the liberal arts and sciences—for people pursuing careers in university teaching and scientific research. This conventional wisdom deserves scrutiny.

Why Change and Innovation in Graduate and Professional Education?

Our legacy of distinction has served us well, and reluctant accommodation within public research universities has not been without merit. In contrast to many less prestigious institutions, research universities have been much more measured in introducing certain changes and reforms for increasing enrollment that have been at the expense of program quality. Yet, for two fundamental reasons, I believe that the dawn of a new millennium is a propitious time to seriously consider change and innovation in graduate and professional education—both across and within programs—in public research universities.

First, as further diminution in financial resources looms large and new revenues are needed, change and innovation that responds to market demands and opportunities (including nascent as well as explicit customer needs) is needed both in the short- and long-term. Why? For the foreseeable future, the financial picture of graduate and professional education in public research universities is threatened in significant ways: probable further declines in federal and state support along with growing public accountability; the tightening of the academic labor market and the contraction of doctoral education; and the likely diminution of revenue streams from other countries—not to mention inexpensive graduate student labor—owing particularly to flux in Asian economies and resulting declines in the huge number of international students now enrolled as graduate students in this country. In the context of such threats, the traditional pattern of reluctant accommodation to market demands and customer needs will likely prove insufficient to meet financial needs. Instead of adaptation, adjustment, and accommodation, our public universities need to reach out to new sources of revenue. Change and innovation that enables us to be more responsive to potential markets and the needs of our customers—both current and prospective students—can go a long way toward helping to ensure a solid financial foundation for the future.

Second, in order to maintain our support and legitimacy over time from various segments of the public and external constituencies, we will need to enact change and innovation that is responsive to emerging societal needs. In the immediate future, for example, the demographic transformation of this nation, coupled with massive cultural and economic changes, invites us to introduce new programs and strengthen existing ones in ways that will better enable diverse workers to contribute to economic growth in the nonuniversity workplace and equip them with skills important for a life of continuing learning and retraining. In particular, programs that fuse professional education and liberal learning are clearly needed to serve the economy and the future workforce, as well as to enrich public life. What John Gardner once said about democracy applies no less to public universities: "Freedom and responsibility, liberty and duty, that's the deal." Change and innovation that better enables us to continue to fulfill our responsibilities to society—our state as well as nation—can go a long way toward fulfilling our obligation to meet our end of the "deal."

A Template for Change and Innovation

In the remainder of the chapter, I advance five proposals for change and innovation in graduate and professional education in public research universities. For each, I sketch and briefly defend the proposal as well as indicate how, and by whom, it might be implemented. Many of the ideas and examples discussed are drawn not only from the University of Wisconsin–Madison and its peer institutions, but also from outside its relatively small peer group of major public research universities.

Developing and Nourishing "Cultures" That Create Opportunities for Change and Innovation

For reasons discussed above, public research universities need to launch initiatives to transcend the legacy of reluctant accommodation to change and innovation in graduate and professional education. To that end, I propose that both administrators as well as faculty focus on developing and maintaining "cultures"—both across and within programs—that invite and encourage administrators and faculty to actively explore opportunities for change. As elaborated below, such changes might range from developing new interdisciplinary programs that respond to the needs of surrounding communities to reinventing traditional degree programs through introducing alternative learning formats such as satellite instruction.

Most public research universities have traditionally looked to faculty as the major source of reform. The explanation is straightforward: Faculty expertise, especially as it is legitimized in original research, supports a folklore that holds that administrators exist primarily to serve the faculty (and, of course, students). Indeed, faculty initiatives often have been the source of change and innovation in graduate education. For example, at the University of Wisconsin–Madison, the development of a highly regarded interdisciplinary master's program in environmental studies was due largely to faculty initiative.

While bottom-up faculty initiatives have great merit, leaving change and innovation to the faculty—unaccompanied by substantial administrative involvement—is limiting. The majority of faculty not only give their major allegiance to Ph.D. programs and their discipline or field of study—and university reward structures support these two allegiances—but they have strong vested interests in the status quo. Faculty are often opponents of change rather than sources of innovation. Furthermore, most faculty simply do not take the time to see the "big picture" of graduate and professional education. As such, they seldom concern themselves with seizing opportunities to establish, for example, new interdisciplinary master's programs that respond to nascent external needs in the community, state, or nation. For these reasons, it is no wonder that many potential changes and innovations, including those that fall outside the Ph.D. orbit and traditional academic disciplines—especially in the liberal arts and sciences—often find no spokesperson on the faculty. In the meantime, entrepreneurs at institutions outside of major research universities often introduce innovations that respond to emerging societal needs long before those in research universities even begin to consider the possibility.

In the twenty-first century, especially in light of rapid changes in the environment, it is imperative that administrators—from the departmental to senior administrative levels—join with faculty in pursuing initiatives for change and innovation and, in so doing, creating "cultures" that advance changes that not only bring in needed revenue but also respond to compelling societal needs. A good example of such administrative leadership comes from our own campus in the past year. David Ward, the chancellor of the University of Wisconsin–Madison, initiated an interdepartmental strategic hiring plan designed to promote cross-departmental and cross-college connections while preparing for growth in academic fields that extend beyond traditional areas of study. Ninety-five proposals were submitted by faculty, with roughly twelve new faculty expected to be hired in clusters of three or four that combine the resources of multiple departments. Initiatives such as this "cluster hiring initiative"—initiatives taken by administrators and faculty that establish and nourish cultures supporting change and innovation—can go a long way in remaking the landscape of graduate and professional education in order to not only strengthen higher learning but to contribute to the larger society as well.

Enlarging Purposes by Serving Students Pursuing Careers in the Nonuniversity Workplace

Although preparing people for advanced professional education at the master's level has taken on greater emphasis in recent years, preparing people for university careers and careers in scientific research—especially at the doctoral level in the liberal arts and sciences—continues to receive much more support in public research universities. Faculty continue to receive significant reward for their participation at the doctoral level, rewards that include smaller course loads and larger salaries. An additional benefit of being associated with doctoral programs is the fact that these programs receive relatively more funding than at any other degree level. Finally, students in most professional fields—save in fields such as business and engineering, where significant amounts of external revenues are received—are generally treated as second-class citizens by many faculty and administrators throughout public research universities.

Especially given the mandate public institutions have received to be responsive to various populations, and to do so within the context of looming financial challenges, it is long past time for public research universities to enlarge their purposes by serving students pursuing careers outside of universities as seriously as they serve doctoral students pursuing careers in academe and scientific research. Pursuing this agenda would address the inequity stated above, that students in professional programs not pursuing academic careers, along with faculty who teach in these programs, generally receive second-class treatment in ways both subtle and not-so-subtle. Such an expansion has significant implications for change and innovation in graduate and professional education. Perhaps most important, as elaborated below, it would mean significantly enhancing program offerings at the post-baccalaureate and master's levels along with introducing nondegree programs that provide for continuing professional education in nontraditional learning formats. It would also invite fundamental questions surrounding nearly every aspect of graduate and professional education, from how faculty reward structures might be modified to altering institutional reward structures.

Enlarging purposes will surely have major effects on the student clientele in graduate and professional education. Since women, minorities, people of color, people working outside the university, part-time students, and students with lower socioeconomic backgrounds are likely to enroll in nondoctoral professional programs disproportionately for the foreseeable future, it is scarcely debatable that placing more emphasis on preparing students for nonuniversity careers will significantly diversify the composition of student bodies in public research universities. Indeed, enlarging purposes, coupled with changes and innovations that give expression to this agenda, is likely to make a major contribution to one of the most oft-articulated goal in public research universities: diversifying student clientele.

Enhancing Program Offerings—Including Interdisciplinary and Nondegree Programs—at all Graduate Levels for Students Pursuing Nonuniversity Careers

If purposes are to be enlarged and the needs of diverse students pursuing nonuniversity careers taken more seriously, program enhancement in professional fields needs to be at the forefront of agendas for change and innovation in graduate and professional education. Four faces of program innovation in professional education are especially important to this effort: introducing new degree programs at the master's and first professional levels; introducing non-degree, certificate programs at the postbaccalaureate level; introducing new interdisciplinary programs throughout graduate and professional education; and strengthening connections between programs in professional fields and programs in the liberal arts and sciences

A starting point for enhancing program offerings is the introduction of new master's programs in emerging fields, including new interdisciplinary fields of study—such as computational biology—designed to update the knowledge and skills of practicing professionals as well as new first-professional degree programs. Regarding the latter, in recent years there has been an increase in the number of first professional degrees in fields such as pharmacy.

Pharmacy, to illustrate, has recently made the the Doctor of Pharmacy (Pharm. D.) the first professional degree in the field. As other professions move beyond the baccalaureate degree as the required entry-level professional degree in the workplace, public

118

research universities are in an enviable position for introducing new programs in such fields. Given their considerable resources—human and financial—public research universities have the expertise and wherewithal to provide leadership in introducing such programs rather than waiting until after nonresearch universities have addressed this need.

Another face of program enhancement concerns the introduction of non-degree, certificate programs at the postbaccalaureate level that are designed for students whose professional and personal lives can be enriched by post-baccalaureate education outside of master's or doctoral programs. The University of Wisconsin–Madison has been one of a small number of universities taking initiative in this regard. To wit, under the leadership of the chancellor and the dean of the Graduate School, Wisconsin will soon fund a handful of cross-campus proposals designed to address the needs of individuals in a variety of professional careers. These new programs, according to the chancellor, offer several major benefits to students: an educational transition for undergraduates from the liberal arts to explore professional opportunities; multidisciplinary breadth that adds perspective to the undergraduate major; and lifelong learning opportunities for professionals to build on their careers. Such programs, especially when they are coupled with distance technology and other off-campus learning formats, provide a promising window of opportunity for public research universities to better serve their various publics.

Still another face of program enhancement concerns the introduction of new interdisciplinary programs throughout graduate and professional education—from postbaccalaureate programs through doctoral programs—designed to meet the needs of working professionals. To illustrate, the University of Colorado-Boulder offers interdisciplinary certificate degree programs in such areas as cognitive science, behavioral genetics, environmental policy, and biotechnology. At the University of Southern California, faculty are currently developing new interdisciplinary professional master's programs—all intended to meet the demands of graduate students and employers by involving employers in the design of the programs—in such fields as computational biology, physics for business applications, and environmental science and technology. And at the Massachusetts Institute of Technology, an interdisciplinary master's degree program in geosystems engineering has been introduced.

Finally, and in the same spirit as interdisciplinary programs, stronger connections between programs in professional fields and programs in the liberal arts and sciences are critically important for students pursuing nonuniversity careers. One of many examples of progress in this direction comes from the flagship campus of the University of Wisconsin. Under the leadership of faculty and administrators, the School of Business has recently introduced a number of program changes at the master's level that incorporate courses from the liberal arts and sciences at the university. To wit, their master's program in arts administration requires students to take several courses in the arts and sciences; students in the MBA program are sometimes required to take foreign language courses; and student-designed programs at the master's level frequently include courses in the liberal arts and sciences. Needless to say, such initiatives—especially those that build on the university's historic and continuing legacy of depth and breadth in the liberal arts and sciences—can contribute to enriching program offerings for students returning to careers in the nonuniversity workplace and, along the way, undermining the pointless dualism between liberal and professional education that continues to this day.

If these four faces of program enhancement are to be realized consonant with strengthening the learning opportunities of students pursuing nonuniversity careers, administrative and faculty initiatives in these directions will clearly be needed. Significantly, faculty in the liberal arts and sciences may often have the most to gain in taking on such innovations—especially in light of the crowded job market for Ph.D.s in many fields—and administrators can greatly enhance the responsiveness of their institutions by strengthening programs in ways that better prepare students for the nonuniversity workplace. Faculty in professional programs can enrich the professional education opportunities of individuals pursuing professional careers outside of the university.

Enhancing Programs in Ways that Strengthen Program Quality and Flexibility

While enlarging purposes and enhancing program offerings can go a long way toward improving the overall landscape of graduate and professional education, change and innovation is no less needed within individual programs—including not only programs designed to prepare people for careers in university teaching but also those designed to prepare people for careers outside of the university. In many graduate and professional programs, change and innovation are needed to strengthen program quality and to strengthen program flexibility.

While there are a number of changes and innovations that can strengthen program quality, three ways to encourage students and faculty alike to invest more heavily in their own as well as in other program participants' teaching and learning—arguably a key touchstone of high-quality programs—find mention here.[1] For one, faculty can encourage much greater "collaborative peer learning" among students *directly* (through in- and out-of-class learning opportunities that encourage such learning), and *indirectly* (through modeling peer learning through their own engagement in collaborative research and team-teaching). By emphasizing collaboration rather than competition, peer learning can significantly improve students' interpersonal and teamwork skills as well as their ability to learn from/through others—skills that can be invaluable to them whether they pursue careers in academe or in the nonuniversity workplace.

Establishing "professional residencies" for students is another way to strengthen programs. Anchored in an applied setting involving intensive, hands-on learning that usually lasts at least one term, residencies can take any number of forms: research and teaching assistantships for students pursuing academic careers; internships in government agencies or businesses or human service organizations; or practica in health care and educational settings. Especially if feedback is regularly provided, professional residencies can greatly help students build bridges between what they learn in class and the "real world;" enable them to develop much deeper and integrated understandings of their professions; and, along the way, help them to strengthen their professional identities.

Still another way to strengthen programs is to require students to complete a "tangible product" such as a thesis, project, report, or creative performance. While virtually all doctoral programs continue to require a capstone product, most master's and other nondoctoral programs no longer have such a requirement. The absence of such a requirement, especially as a culminating activity, is not insignificant. In completing a tangible product, students are challenged to draw upon and knit together relevant principles, practices, and skills learned in their programs to create a product that is valuable to the field as well as personally. One of the most powerful ways to invite students to invest in their learning—and to connect theory with practice—is through developing a "tangible product" for enhancing learning.

To put it gently, program flexibility has not exactly been a hallmark of graduate and professional education in public research universities during the last century. Many research universities have only belatedly and begrudgingly revisited traditional learning formats. While some innovations in program delivery have been around higher education for some time, others are relatively recent. Here, I briefly discuss two potential avenues of innovation, avenues worth exploring if graduate and professional programs in public research universities are to be more responsive to the needs of working professionals: intensive-learning programs and distance education.

In broad strokes, intensive-learning programs are time-intensive programs anchored in compressed learning experiences that are offered through nontraditional learning formats such as weekend, evening, and modular courses as well as through mediated instruction. Since they are designed to meet the needs of part-time students who wish to pursue their education while maintaining their employment, intensive programs can vary not only in terms of learning format but also in terms as such factors as amount of credit for prior learning, number of class contact hours, and use of adjunct faculty. Interestingly, while intensive-learning programs have been rendered largely invisible at research universities, they have become very popular at many regional universities. By way of illustration, Regis University in Colorado has been a national leader in providing intensive-learning programs at the undergraduate as well as graduate level. Regis now offers master's programs in a variety of nontraditional learning formats of varying duration. Master's courses are offered at Regis's main campus, at off-campus centers located at sites such as the local corporate headquarters of U.S. West, and at myriad out-of-state locations.

In the last few years, the information technologies revolution has propelled us toward a global educational network in which knowledge and information will be available any time, any place. Distance education, the first step in this direction, offers enormous possibilities for change and innovation in graduate and professional education. From off-campus courses and correspondence courses to electronic transmission, distance education can be used to deliver courses electronically to sites anywhere in the world. Ironically, given that much of the technology that is fueling distance learning was developed in public research universities, these institutions have been slow to incorporate distance learning into graduate and professional programs. Significantly, it has been in nondoctoral institutions that much of the initiative in distance technology has taken place, as demonstrated in these examples: the new Western Governors University will deliver all courses electronically; the master's programs in engineering offered by National Technological University are delivered by satellite network to nearly four hundred corporate sites nationwide; and Lehigh University offers satellite TV master's and doctoral programs in chemistry. Except for a relatively small number of graduate programs, mostly in the fields of education and engineering, distance technology is not being as widely used by the nation's major public universities as the conventional wisdom suggests.

In the coming years, the major public universities have an enormous opportunity to better serve working students by introducing changes in distance education. While distance education has possibilities at the doctoral level, it is at the postbaccalaureate and master's levels where innovation is the most likely to take root. Especially given the possibilities for individualizing teaching and learning through distance education, as well the opportunities for using distance learning to animate continuing professional education (including nondegree programs), public research universities are long past due in seriously exploring emerging technology to implement distance technologies throughout higher education.

In summary, the suggestions advanced here—from strengthening programs through such changes and innovations as "professional residencies" to innovations for enhancing program flexibility such as distance learning—all contribute to enhancing programs that will redound directly to the benefit of students, that will financially replenish universities, and that will also help to guarantee our responsiveness to agendas for workers with lifelong learning skills who can skillfully connect theory with practice.

Advancing the Concept of "Teaching and Learning Communities" Both Across and Within Programs of Study

Public research universities, and the graduate and professional programs nested within them, can be fruitfully viewed as "teaching and learning communities" in which all participants are engaged in an ongoing search for truth and understanding through the exploration, diffusion, and testing of ideas and truth-claims. Charting a course that few top administrators have been willing to do, the chancellor of the University of Wisconsin–Madison, David Ward, went so far as to advance the concept of "learning community" in his inaugural address. Still, despite the rhetoric about "community" throughout higher education, there are not many indications that there has been significant movement in graduate and professional education to ensure that the idea of community is becoming an important thread in the tapestry of everyday student and faculty life. Many faculty and students continue to lead divided lives, and there have been few visible efforts to enhancing community in graduate and professional education.

If we are to maintain fidelity to universities as being centered around "teaching and learning communities,"—an idea that I believe should be the soul of universities, one which transcends teaching, research, and service—I propose that faculty, administrators, and students begin to discuss more openly what "community" might mean to them and how it might be implemented. To help introduce such discussions, let me suggest that our communities should, at a minimum, be:

Communities animated by a shared sense of purpose that is grounded in an ethic of service to others—both within and outside the university. This ethic transcends the specific agendas of the community and its members while respecting individual differences.

Intellectual and moral communities that maintain fidelity to truth-seeking and the advancement of knowledge through preserving freedom of inquiry and expression; encouraging risk-taking; maintaining the highest intellectual, professional, and ethical standards; preserving the salience of evidence, reason, and disciplined discourse; and, by valuing differences and welcoming open disagreement and criticism, are committed to the continuous questioning of orthodoxies, dogmas, authorities, and accepted truths.

Collaborative communities that are anchored in the belief that teaching and learning can often be immeasurably enriched through collaboration: collaborative inquiry, shared leadership, investments in one another's growth and development, and partnerships that enrich the lives of not only students and faculty but those of external stakeholders as well.

Communities of differences that value wholeness and view differences—among individuals as well across groups—as vital to enriching teaching and learning. These communities seek diversity in membership and continually draw upon differences in cultural background, race, gender, age, sexual orientation, life experiences, ways-of-knowing, and perspective.

Inclusive communities that emphasize wholeness and treat all participants (from faculty and students to administrators and staff) as teachers as well as learners and that invite external constituencies to actively participate.

Human, caring communities that celebrate human values—compassion and understanding, non-exploitativeness, trust and support, respect for the dignity of others, human commitment—and use humor and laughter and simple acts of human kindness and hospitality to nurture a caring environment in which all members feel a sense of belonging and place.

Responsive communities that are sensitive not only to faculty, students, and administrators, but also to external constituencies and to the needs compatible with the mission of universities.

Defining "community" across and within graduate and professional programs is one thing; giving expression to that definition is another. Inviting students and administrators, along with faculty, to assume individual and collective responsibility for operationalizing as well as defining the concept is imperative if our graduate and professional programs are to embrace "teaching and learning communities" and give them more meaning than a slogan. In building communities that graduates want to return to over the course of their lifetimes, we will not only enhance our reputation among employers and prospective students but we will provide learning experiences that redound to the benefit of society in the form of a more educated workforce and enlightened citizenry.

Roots and Wings: Transforming Graduate and Professional Education

Notwithstanding their unparalleled reputation both for advancing knowledge and providing high-quality advanced training, our nation's public research universities have only gradually, and often reluctantly, advanced change and innovation in graduate and professional education. In light of the challenges of the twenty-first century, including not only financial ones but also growing public doubt about our willingness to be responsive to emerging societal needs, the time has come to move beyond a century in which post-baccalaureate and master's education is viewed as ancillary to doctoral education, and in which professional education is viewed as inferior to education in the liberal arts and sciences.

Public research universities need to complete the transformation of graduate education—a transformation in which nondoctoral education is no longer viewed as second-class and, no less important, in which there is no hierarchy or antagonism between the liberal arts and sciences and professional fields of study. To that end, I have made some suggestions for change and innovation that are anchored in an enlargement of purposes and enhancement of program offerings—across degree and nondegree levels—for students pursuing nonuniversity as well as university careers.

Consonant with the proposals advanced here, I conclude by suggesting some corollary challenges that also deserve our consideration:

- What should the relationship be between the research mission of public research universities and graduate and professional training?
- Who should we serve? How can we identify our clientele—in graduate and professional programs?
- What should the balance and symmetry be between master's, first-professional, and doctoral programs—as well as between nondegree, postbaccalaureate programs?

- To what extent, and how, should the historic connection of advanced study and research be revisited—even disrupted—in non-Ph.D. programs and professional programs?
- Along with any major changes in graduate and professional education, what are the major implications for the training of faculty, for faculty roles and responsibilities, for faculty reward structures?

Addressing such questions can help us prepare to engage in change and innovation that maintains our legacy of distinction. At the same time, we can effectively prepare for an uncertain future in ways that preserve our financial integrity while enhancing our responsiveness to the larger society we serve.

Note

1. I draw here not only my experiences in higher education over the last several decades but also on the nearly 800 interviews that my colleagues and I conducted with six stakeholder groups (faculty, students, program alumni, program administrators, university administrators, and employers) as part of a national study of master's programs that looked in-depth at 47 programs in 11 fields representing both the liberal arts and sciences and professional fields. The two books resulting from the study are listed in the references below.

Bibliography

Conrad, Clifton F., Jennifer Grant Haworth, and Susan Bolyard Millar. *A Silent Success: Master's Education in the United States*. Baltimore: Johns Hopkins University Press, 1993.

Haworth, Jennifer Grant, and Clifton F. Conrad. *Emblems of Quality: Developing and Sustaining High-Quality Programs*. Boston: Allyn and Bacon, 1997.

The Future of International Studies

David M. Trubek

IF YOU WANTED TO LEARN about Thailand, the campus of the University of Wisconsin–Madison would be a good place to start. In Dane County, Wisconsin, far from any major port, national capital, or major financial center, you will find experts on Thai history, politics, language, society, and economy. You will find scientists who are working closely with Thai counterparts on basic and applied research. You could meet a number of UW students specializing in Thai studies, most of whom have spent a year or more in Thailand. You can meet and talk to any of the one hundred or so Thai students and visiting scholars currently in residence. Go to the alumni office and they will provide you with information on the active, four hundred-person-strong Wisconsin Alumni Association of Thailand. The library has an excellent collection of Thai materials. UW–Madison faculty visit Thailand regularly, and the chancellor has visited Bangkok twice in the last few years.

This story can be repeated substituting any region of the world, or many countries large and small, for Thailand. Name your country and it is likely that the UW–Madison teaches its languages, studies its history and contemporary affairs, investigates its role in international trade and politics, sends students there for advanced training, has ties to its universities, and trains some of its future scholars and leaders. We regularly teach forty different

David M. Trubek is dean of International Studies at the University of Wisconsin–Madison.

languages each year, and offer another twenty on an occasional basis. We have interdisciplinary programs covering all the world's regions and regularly offer our students overseas experiences in thirty countries. We have hundreds of faculty members with in-depth international expertise. We have formal relationships with several hundred universities around the world. Upwards of one thousand scholars from all over the world come to Madison each year to work with our faculty and interact with our students.

International education begins with in-depth knowledge of the countries and regions of the world. But it does not stop there: we also study and teach about issues that transcend countries and even regions. Do you want to learn about commonalities in the literatures of former British colonies? The spread of nationalism and ethnic violence in many parts of the world? The role of the United Nations in peacekeeping? The relationship between African-Americans and Africa? What about the management of global financial markets or the impact of economic globalization on workers and wages? You'll find research groups on the Madison campus working on these questions, and you can enroll in courses that explore these and other contemporary issues.

Look at the student body. Most of our undergraduates develop competence in at least one foreign language. The interdisciplinary undergraduate major in international studies, with close to four hundred students, is one of the largest majors on campus. A large percentage of students in the College of Letters and Science specialize in international topics, major in foreign languages, or spend at least one semester studying overseas. And many do all three. Several hundred graduate students are enrolled in programs in international studies, and many of them being trained as specialists who will conduct advanced research and train future generations. Increasingly, international studies are becoming *de rigeur* for students in professional schools of business, law, agriculture, engineering, and the health sciences.

Travel around to any of America's research universities and the same story will repeat itself. There is nothing unique about the

Wisconsin experience. All of our major universities have made substantial commitments to international education. They have added numerous international specialists to their faculties, incorporated international topics in the curriculum at all levels, provided support for students who wish to develop international skills, built relations with foreign universities, and established linkages with public and private institutions that need knowledge about the world outside the United States.

To this end, they have all made major changes in university structure and organization. During the course of the twentieth century, all the research universities created specialized institutions that are dedicated to developing and transmitting knowledge about the rest of the world and maintaining linkages between the university and institutions here and abroad. Taken together, these institutions constitute the *international education complexes* of the research universities. They organize specialized courses, provide advice for students seeking international learning and careers, support faculty teaching and research, maintain relations with foreign universities, and provide international information to policymakers and the public.

Of course, emphasis varies from one institution to another, as do organizational forms. Some universities stress regional studies while others have focused more on topical issues like arms control and global warming. Some aspire to comprehensive coverage while others have concentrated on specific regions of the world. On some campuses the international complex is highly decentralized and dispersed; on others there are offices, centers, or institutes that serve as central support and coordination mechanisms. But whatever the focus and whatever the form, these complexes have been assembled to build and maintain linkages between the traditional structure of the American university and the sources and consumers of international knowledge. They facilitate both the formation and the dissemination of learning about the world and America's role in the world.

Our university international education complexes are the

envy of educators from other countries. Each of our campuses has been able to assemble large numbers of specialists on world regions and global issues. Usually, they have systems of administrative and financial support that enrich scholarly life for faculty and students alike. There are specialized advising services and fellowships for students, and research grants and travel awards for faculty. Colloquia, workshops, and speaker series are available to all. The campuses maintain linkages of one kind or another with universities and research centers around the world. In some cases, they also have connections to domestic policymakers, international organizations, international business, and transnational nongovernmental organizations. Few university campuses elsewhere in the world boast comparable resources and capabilities.

International Studies at Century's End: Turbulence, Debate, and Doubts

This is a time of great turbulence and ferment in international studies at our research universities. Because international education serves as a link between the university and world society, it is susceptible to changes in both. And today, dramatic changes are occurring both in world society and in American universities. The international education community must deal with changed universities, new types of students, and a transformed world scene. It is being forced to rethink both its mission and its methods.

This has led to a great deal of internal debate and no shortage of concern and disquiet. As the community looks ahead to the next century, it is unsure of its future and divided in its counsels. Some predict a decline in the strength and importance of international education on U.S. campuses, while others see the dawn of a new age with great prospects for growth and improvement. Some argue that as a result of globalization and post-Cold War international politics, we need to make radical changes in curriculum and organization. A few go so far as to suggest that we should replace area studies with global studies, and shift our policy focus completely from geopolitics to geoeconomics. Others see "global studies" and similar efforts to respond to a changing world as a passing fad and urge that priority be given to preservation of existing capabilities. Some think that the most pressing need is to strengthen the role of the humanities in international education, while others think social science and professional training should be the top priority.

Behind the debates between optimists and pessimists, regionalists and globalists, traditionalists and reformers, humanists and social scientists, one can detect a shared concern for the fragility of the enterprise and the sustainability of the international education complexes that have grown up on our campuses. These institutions have been built by hard work, sustained by intellectual excitement, and supported by academic leaders and external agencies. Many are flourishing today. But all are being buffeted by forces from on- and off-campus: these forces threaten the foundations on which our contemporary international complexes have been constructed. What seemed like a permanent change on the American campus now looks more evanescent. For the first time in fifty years, international educators fear that the capabilities built up so carefully over many decades may be at risk.

I share these concerns. I am proud of what has been accomplished at Wisconsin and in our sister universities. I am hopeful for the future but I recognize that we face tremendous challenges. I think we have begun to confront these difficulties and are devising imaginative responses to the changes occurring around us. But no one should be complacent: more has to be done at all levels inside and outside the university to ensure the continuity and the growth of international studies in our research universities.

In this chapter I outline the current situation and suggest ways the international education community can overcome the challenges we all face. I draw heavily on my experiences as a faculty member and dean of international studies at the University of Wisconsin–Madison. I will report on some of the efforts underway on the Madison campus, relay information from contacts with other universities in the United States and overseas, and outline the issues common to all large public research universities and to other institutions of higher education at the end of this century.

How We Got Here

International education is nothing new. American universities have been oriented toward the rest of the world and connected to institutions overseas from the beginning. In particular, scholars in the humanities have always been interested in the study of foreign languages, literatures, and the great world civilizations. World War II, however, marked a watershed in the development of international studies in this country and started a shift from an emphasis on humanistic knowledge to one that included development of practical knowledge for policymaking. Changes begun during the war accelerated in the post-World War II period, and they help account for the formation of international studies as we know it today.

During World War II the U.S. national security establishment found itself in a global conflict that involved operations literally in every part of the world. Government recognized the need for trained personnel with language and area knowledge. Although the universities contained people with these skills, their numbers were small, especially relative to the perceived need. Moreover, while there was substantial expertise on Europe, there were relatively few people who studied other parts of the world. Even when experts on places like India, China, Arabia, and Africa existed, many of them were concerned more with ancient civilizations and dead languages than with contemporary speech and immediate social and political issues. While war-inspired crash programs helped fill the immediate need, the American establishment emerged from the war with a sense that our universities were not equipped to produce the international expertise needed for the country's newly-found global responsibilities. Voices were heard urging restructuring and expansion of international education for the postwar world.

The Postwar Boom in International Studies

International studies flourished in the postwar period. It was fed by forces internal to the universities and support from outside. Forward-looking educators saw international studies as a promising area for development. Partly inspired by wartime experiences, scholars in the social sciences had awakened to the need both for comparative knowledge and for insights relevant to international policy concerns. Thus they were eager to add experts on world regions to their departments. Historians saw the possibility of expanding beyond the triad of America, Europe, and the Ancient World that dominated curricula in the first half of the century. Similar opportunities were presented to language teachers when universities saw the need for instruction in a whole range of languages that had not been taught at all or were only offered in a few places for advanced specialists. Everyone thrilled to the possibility of constructing knowledge that might be useful to policymakers. The challenges of global security and Third World development offered rich opportunities for policy-oriented social science. Educators at the research universities saw the emergence of a new market for their graduate students as the postwar "internationalization" wave spread quickly throughout the college and university sector, creating a constant demand for trained specialists who could both teach in conventional disciplines and also provide education about all the regions of the world.

The Cold War lent urgency to the project of expanding international studies, stimulated government interest in university developments, and offered a focus for energy. Confronting what they thought would be a protracted global struggle with the Soviet Union, the People's Republic of China, and their allies, the American elite saw the need to institutionalize the temporary relationship between national security and the academy that had been forged on an emergency basis during the hot war. Major foundations like Ford and Rockefeller began to invest heavily in international studies. They were followed by the federal government, which developed programs to support foreign area and language studies in the research universities. These were designed to produce and sustain expertise about the societies, cultures, economies, and languages of all the world's regions. This meant increasing the study of modern languages, especially the languages of potential enemies and possible allies. It meant developing more area expertise within the social sciences. It meant bringing language, cultural, and social studies together to develop a more holistic understanding of events in specific countries and regions.

Universities responded to these opportunities with relative ease. Thanks in part to the GI Bill, the postwar period was one of rapid growth in tertiary education. Public universities like Wisconsin grew dramatically. There were opportunities to hire large numbers of new faculty, thus permitting the universities to expand existing international programs and create many new ones. There was growing student interest in international subjects. World War II had expanded the global awareness of the American public. As a result of the Cold War and the overseas expansion of the U.S. economy, there were more prospects for international careers. The supply of international experts on faculties grew rapidly to meet existing demand and to exploit opportunities to create further demand for their teaching, research, and service.

Even though the boom in international studies was facilitated by national concerns and geopolitical interests, by and large the universities maintained their autonomy from the national security apparatus and often became centers of criticism of U.S. foreign policy. The interest in expanding international studies arose from core concerns of major academic disciplines, and international scholars were supported by core university resources as well as by extramural sources. Traditions of academic freedom encouraged wide-ranging inquiry and vigorous criticism of public policy. So while Cold War concerns had a real impact on the campuses, and external funding affected priorities, the universities never became mere instruments of government policy.

Area Studies Centers and the Emergence of the International Education Complex

Initially, at least in places like the UW–Madison, attention was focused on the creation of what came to be called "area studies"—an in-depth, holistic, interdisciplinary approach to understanding specific world regions. Of course, many universities had been committed to the study of other parts of the world long before the onset of the Cold War, so that area studies was in some way the continuation, on a much enlarged basis, of earlier traditions. But area studies did not just enlarge the scale of these programs; it also involved a major change in focus. Earlier, humanistic studies were supplemented—if not sometimes replaced—by a focus on contemporary social, economic, and political issues. The postwar area studies movement was based on a belief, then quite strong in the social sciences, in the *interdependence* of knowledge in the social disciplines. That is, people believed that insights in any discipline would depend in part on knowledge to be gleaned from specialists in another. Political scientists believed that breakthroughs in comparative politics could not occur without knowledge of the economies and cultures of the countries under scrutiny; economists thought that economic development involved changes in culture and systems of governance as well as in business behavior. Everyone agreed that a student could not really understand a country without knowing its language, history, and cultural traditions, or without living there.

For those reasons, scholars everywhere supported the creation of new institutions that would foster interdisciplinary communication and cooperation and organize curricula in new ways. These centers would bring specialists from various fields together; organize new curricular offerings that would provide students with comprehensive programs combining language training with studies in the humanistic and social disciplines; and create opportunities for students to spend time in the region of their specialization. Hence the creation of organized "area studies centers," which served to build holistic knowledge of world regions and create organized curricula and new majors, minors, master's programs, and other specialized credentials for area studies students.

Driven by faculty energy and excitement and the support of forward-looking administrators, and heavily supported by extramural funding from foundations and the federal government, these centers flourished on many campuses. In a time of rapid growth of the university, it proved relatively easy to assemble people from many disciplines who wanted to study developments in places like Latin America, the Soviet Union, or Asia, and who were eager to work with others having similar interests. At Madison, and on many other research university campuses, these area studies centers were the nucleus for the emergence of large complexes of specialized centers, programs, and institutes dedicated to international education. These institutional complexes existed in creative tension with traditional departments. They maintained close ties to scholars and institutions in the regions they studied. In some cases they developed linkages to policymakers.

From Area Studies to Global Studies: The Growth of the International Education Complex

Area studies centers often were the primary nucleus for today's large international education complexes. Over time, however, other major dimensions have been added so that today's typical research university now contains a wide range of specialized international educational offerings, ranging from undergraduate majors to interdisciplinary Ph.D. programs. Most also have large organized interdisciplinary international research enterprises, and many have outreach programs and other service operations.

These varied teaching, research, and service activities, and the institutions that support them, constitute the international education "complexes" that form such a unique feature of research universities like the UW–Madison. In addition to interdisciplinary centers for the study of specific world regions (e.g., Latin American studies, Asian studies, European studies), there are many other types of specialized international units. Most campuses also have interdisciplinary centers organized on a topical rather than a geographic and cultural basis. These include centers on topics like arms control and disarmament, development and economic growth, and human rights. Increasingly, we see the emergence of centers of "global studies," which expand the scale of "area studies" to embrace world society, economy, and politics. Many universities also have units devoted to international issues unique to a given discipline or professional field such as international business, economics, or legal studies: for example, the UW–Madison has a Center for International Business Education and Research, an East Asian Legal Studies Center, and a Law and Globalization program. Some universities have specialized "study abroad" units designed to encourage students to include overseas study and work in their academic programs, as well as offices that provide specialized services for the increasing numbers of international students in all fields enrolled at the research universities. Many campuses have specialized "outreach" offices that disseminate international knowledge to the K–12 system, other colleges and universities, and the general public. And some schools have units whose mission is to provide technical assistance to developing countries.

The International Education Complex and the Traditional Structure of the University

The growth of international education complexes in the postwar period changed the landscape of many campuses throughout the United States. All of a sudden, new majors were defined based on regions (Latin American studies and Asian studies) or around topics (international relations or development). Instead of being limited to majoring in economics, political Science, Spanish, or sociology, students could select one of these new sets of offerings in addition to—or instead of—the more traditional fields. And along with these changes in the curriculum came organizational changes as new offices, centers, programs, and institutes that had not

not existed before were added to manage the new courses, majors, research programs, and service activities. This brought to the fore the issue of the relations between the new structures and the established institutions on campus.

An Alternative Axis

From the point of view of the traditional structure of the American university, this complex of internationally oriented and largely interdisciplinary institutions offers an *alternative axis of organization.* Where the traditional axis is built around disciplinary departments organized into largely autonomous colleges, the international education complex cuts across departmental and college lines. International knowledge requires inputs from many fields, so the area, topical, and global studies centers typically draw people from many colleges and dozens of departments. Because overseas experiences can enrich almost any field of study, the study-abroad offices usually serve students who are pursuing a wide range of majors and careers, from anthropology and business to water resource management and zoology. Similarly, policy analysis, technical assistance, and outreach usually require holistic knowledge and the services of faculty and staff from several fields. Because so much of international education demands services that combine input from several disciplines, universities built separate international studies structures that complement the historical axis of organization. Some of these structures challenged traditional boundaries.

Different Methods and New Missions

The international education complexes not only represent an alternative axis for the organization of academic services, they also redefine the way the university should fulfill its traditional mission of training students and producing knowledge. Study abroad, for example, exists because educators decided that to acquire a language and understand a culture, long-term residence in another country was superior to simply sitting in a classroom somewhere in the United States. Area studies emerged because people believed in the interdependence of social knowledge and assumed that no single discipline could provide the insights and understandings needed to deal with issues in other countries. Thus it was thought that even if your primary interest was in the Brazilian *economy*, you could not understand it unless you could read and speak Portuguese and had a grasp of the nation's history and politics. More recently, people have also seen the need to supplement interdisciplinary studies of nations and regions with an understanding of broader forces and phenomena, so the study of a subject like the Brazilian economy now also requires an understanding of global capital flows, the emerging world trade regime, and the global shifts in ideas about the role of the state in the economy.

Further, international education represents a significant expansion of the traditional mission of the university. To be sure, the primary role of international studies is to strengthen and expand the university's capacity to produce knowledge and educate students. But the international education complexes also support the direct provision of policy advice; the dissemination of information beyond the campus to the public, K–12 system, and business; the development of universities and other institutions overseas; and similar new missions. This expanded mission had not been contemplated when the UW–Madison was founded 150 years ago, and was only beginning to be recognized when it celebrated its one hundredth anniversary in 1949.

Useful Supplement or Dangerous Rival: The Traditional Axis and the International Complex

The size of the international complexes vary from university to university. In some cases, they are very large and engage large numbers of students and faculty. At the UW–Madison campus the international education complex is embedded in separate traditional schools and colleges. However, if all the UW–Madison's international faculty and staff who are now housed in various colleges were to be formally joined together, the resulting "international college" would have hundreds of faculty members, teach thousands of students, and be larger than all but the biggest of the traditional units.

Today the international complexes exist in complex tension with the units that form the older and more traditional axis of university organization. While most educators recognize that the specialized interdisciplinary and cross-college units that make up these complexes are useful if not essential supplements to traditional campus structures, some perceive them as dangerous rivals. Where most see these institutions as enriching disciplines and enhancing the capacities of departments, others see them as competitors for student enrollments, academic prestige, faculty loyalties, and campus resources.

While it is easy to see why conflict might erupt between international studies and traditional units, there was very little tension during the postwar boom. For several reasons, the potential conflict between the disciplinary axis and interdisciplinary international studies was kept under control. Universities favored internationalization and disciplines promoted international study. The social sciences recognized the importance of international knowledge and the interdependence of international studies. Professors sought opportunities to conduct research, teach, and provide advice around the world. First the language departments and then other disciplines recognized the importance of overseas experiences. Few worried about competition for scarce resources because there was no real scarcity: in an era of rapid growth there seemed to be enough to go around for everyone. This was especially true because international education received substantial support from external sources, principally the federal government and the major private foundations. The existence of extramural resources available exclusively for international education made it easier to develop new programs and thus create an alternative axis of campus organization without generating too much conflict with established units.

Challenges at the End of the Century

Two questions face international education on our campuses today. Can the era of good will continue in a different intellectual climate and a period of relative austerity? And can international education change fast enough to meet all the new needs of students and the public? These questions have emerged due to the rapid and unexpected changes—changes both occurring throughout the world that international educators relate to and within the universities they serve. Poised between a world in turbulence and universities undergoing significant changes, international educators are reassessing their missions, reengineering their institutions, and seeking new bases of intellectual and material support. The UW–Madison, like many of its peers, has spent a good part of the last decade reviewing the international education complex, restructuring some units and creating new programs in areas previously underserved.

To understand the new context for international education in universities like the UW–Madison, we have to look closely at three areas of change and turbulence: those occurring in world society; those happening on university campuses; and those affecting the extramural funding sources that have been so vital to international education in the past. The changes in all these areas during the past decade have been rapid and dramatic. We are still struggling to respond to them.

Changes in World Society

At the dawn of the twenty-first century, the world looks very different than it did even a scant twenty years ago. Changes too numerous to mention have taken place, but a few seem to be particularly central to the changing context for international studies. These are the end of the Cold War, globalization of the economy, the communications revolution, cultural conflict and the "clash among civilizations," and the changing role of the United States in world politics and the world economy.

The end of the Cold War created new topics for academic

study (like democratization and transitions to a market economy) while rendering others (like the study of communism and nuclear deterrence) less central. It opened up new possibilities for overseas study and research as U.S. universities developed relations with counterparts in places like the former Soviet Union, Eastern Europe, and China. At the same time it seems to have led to declining interest in international affairs in this country and to a reassessment of many government programs, including support for academic exchanges, which had flourished in a period when the U.S. saw itself in an ideological struggle with a major enemy and viewed the universities as allies in this struggle.

The end of the Cold War also coincided with, and facilitated, the most recent wave of economic "globalization." While there has been a world economy for centuries, and although the international economy was highly integrated one hundred years ago, quantitative and qualitative changes in the past twenty years have led many to describe this as a new and different stage of world economic integration. At least four changes mark this era as different: dispersion of manufacturing production from the North to the South and the rise of strong export-oriented economies in many developing countries; a global financial market making capital available throughout the world and constraining national economic policy; the declining importance of nation states in the management and operations of the economy; and the growing importance in the world economy of subnational regions like the American Midwest.

These changes in the world economy and its governance structures have rendered some knowledge bases obsolete and created the need for new knowledge about issues like the operation of the World Trade Organization, the regulation of global financial markets, and the export potential of regions like the Midwest. They have also led to a much greater internationalization of the U.S. economy, as the role of exports and imports in our gross domestic product have soared. This has generated new demands for international knowledge from business and state governments, and for expanded international instruction within professional schools.

A related development is the global communications revolution. The computer, the satellite, and other technical changes have led to better and much cheaper telephonic communications, facilitated the spread of TV, permitted the creation of email, the Internet, and other information technology capacities. The speed and ease with which information and images of all kinds can cross national borders have increased exponentially. This chapter was written in a small and relatively isolated cottage, but while I wrote I kept in contact with people all around the world by email and telephone: these technologies gave me communications capabilities that not even embassies, corporations, or other major institutions could muster fifty years ago when the UW–Madison turned one hundred.

These changes have not only made it possible to link economic actors on a global scale; they also offer tremendous potential for linking individual scholars and universities more generally. Email and the Internet have greatly facilitated scholarly exchanges and research, and universities are beginning to share courses by distance education on a global scale. Yet, while the global communications revolution has created a flood of information that can enrich study and research, it also threatens to overwhelm students and professors alike. The sheer volume of information now easily available creates major problems of quality assessment and organization.

Great changes also result from the emergence or reemergence of ethnic, nationalist, and religiously-based conflicts that have taken place in many parts of the world. The end of the Cold War unleashed nationalist forces in the former Soviet Union and elsewhere: in many cases these are ethnic conflicts as well. At the same time, the global communications revolution and other changes have made it possible to link cultural groups across national boundaries, thus creating new forms of cleavage and new possibilities for global conflict. Some think a resulting "clash of civilizations" will develop and become the new central axis of world politics.

Finally, the end of the Cold War, globalization of the economy, and other changes have led to major shifts in the position and role of the United States in world society. They help explain the growing interest in economic competitiveness and "geo-economic" concerns, as well as waning interest in traditional issues of national security. They probably help account for what looks like a new wave of isolationism in important segments of American society. As the global ideological, material, and military struggle of the Cold War winds down, Americans seem to want to either withdraw from the world, or redefine our international relations along lines of economic conflict.

The renewal of isolationist tendencies and the new emphasis on U.S. economic competitiveness create tremendous challenges for America's universities. We have to be beacons of international interest and understanding in a time when some in the media and the political elite seem to have lost their interest in world affairs. We have to maintain our commitment to the pursuit of universal knowledge and academic autonomy while at the same time providing assistance to those whose primary concern is with the growth of our national economy.

Changes in Universities

Turbulence in world politics has been matched by turbulence on the campus. There have been fiscal, administrative, and intellectual developments that have challenged the academic traditions and institutional organization of the international education complexes. Some of these represent a critique of existing efforts; others a call for new programs to meet underserved needs.

At the intellectual level, a number of critiques address the way international education was practiced in the post–World War II period. In some circles, there has been a collapse of belief in disciplinary interdependence: as a result, some have suggested that the holistic and interdisciplinary methods pioneered by area studies are inadequate to produce truly scientific knowledge. Others who have not questioned the basic interdisciplinary approach have wondered about the continuing relevance of the regional focus, arguing that a global perspective may be more relevant today. A third type of critique has come from people who view much of U.S. scholarship about the rest of the world as being marked by ethnocentric biases. There also has been criticism of the academy's engagement with policymakers on the grounds that the search for policy relevance can compromise objectivity or result in complicity with dubious policies. Conversely, others have labeled international scholarship as irrelevant "mandarin" studies and called for more applied work of immediate practical use to business and government.

A second shockwave has come from the era of fiscal austerity experienced by all public universities and many private schools. Universities like the UW–Madison have seen their budgets cut and have responded by reducing the size of the faculty and student body. This retrenchment has generated the potential for real tension with traditional academic units as deans and departments look for ways to save money and downsize. The large international education complexes may look to some like tempting targets for cutbacks. International educators find themselves struggling to maintain the range and breadth of curricular offerings established in more affluent times, let alone add new courses needed to equip students with the skills demanded by a rapidly changing world scene.

A third set of challenges comes from changes in campus priorities. The most important of these are the growing interest on the research campuses in undergraduate education and the drift of student interest from liberal arts to professional or preprofessional training. While the international education complexes have always included important elements of undergraduate training, and professional schools like law, business, and public policy have paid attention to international education in the past, the center of gravity in international studies at the UW–Madison (as on many other campuses) has been on graduate education in the humanities and social sciences and particularly on producing Ph.Ds. Now, however, with the Ph.D. "market" at best flat and probably in decline, and with new demands for undergraduate and professional education emerging, international educators have been called upon to revise old programs and develop new ones.

Changes in Extramural Support

One of the most serious challenges facing the international education complexes today comes from changes in their sources of extramural support. Not only has there been an overall decline in the funds available from traditional sources like major foundations and the U.S. government, there is also real uncertainty about what kinds of programs might be funded with the money that remains. This is especially true for the foundations, which have been reassessing the nature and purpose of their support for international education. Some traditional supporters of international studies have announced an end to support for area studies as such but have not articulated a clear vision of what forms of international learning and teaching they hope to support in their place. Others call for major changes in area studies without offering a fully articulated new vision. In such a climate, competition for extramural funding has become very keen, funding search costs have gone up, and it is much harder to make long-run plans for projects that are in whole or part dependent on extramural support.

Impact on International Studies: The Emergence of a Twenty-first-Century Vision

Changes in the world, the universities, and the extramural support system have generated both excitement and anxiety among international educators in recent years. This has been a period both of heated debate and creative ferment. Institutions have been forced to adapt to new circumstances. There have been struggles between those who felt the only priority was to preserve existing courses and academic programs and those who emphasized the need for innovation. For many, the process has been painful, but the struggle is beginning to pay off. International educators have begun to cope with the challenges presented by the new context. They have seized new opportunities made possible by some of the intellectual, political, economic, and technological changes now underway. As the twentieth century comes to an end, a new vision of international studies is beginning to emerge at the UW–Madison and on campuses around the nation.

This vision is based on the need to preserve existing strengths while also developing new offerings for new constituencies. It recognizes that the traditionalists and the reformers were both right. In the new vision, the first goal must be to conserve valuable capabilities. These include both intellectual resources and know-how on ways to develop new knowledge and disseminate it to disparate audiences. The in-depth area knowledge and language capacity fostered by the area centers form the foundation for all other types of international study and education. Existing policy centers not only bring together expertise on important contemporary issues; they also know how to transmit relevant knowledge to policymakers and the public. International relations programs provide essential information on foreign policy and the operation of the interstate system. The specialized administrative staffs that support international education have irreplaceable special knowledge about overseas operations, extramural funding, and interdepartmental cooperation. To the extent possible, these assets must be preserved. But conservation alone is not enough. The emerging vision recognizes that it is equally essential to be innovative. To do that, we must refocus on new needs of our students, reimagine international education, restructure the alliances on which this interdisciplinary enterprise is built, and develop new ideas for a changing world.

Refocusing on Students and Their Changing Needs
The first challenge is to rethink what our students need today and

what they will need twenty years from now to operate effectively in the international arena. A much larger percentage of the student body will need to develop international skills in the future than has been the case in the past. As global knowledge and international skills become more important to sectors of U.S. society and the U.S. economy, international educators will have to reach out to a larger and different student constituency. This will not only mean increasing the numbers of students served by our programs, but also changing the programs as well. We are already seeing this process at work in Wisconsin: for example, as exports loom larger in the state economy, government and business have called for new kinds of international education at all levels from K–12 to the doctorate.

While graduate training will continue to be important, and liberal arts will continue be central to international studies, international educators will have to spend more time with undergraduates and with students in the professional disciplines. Moreover, we will need to provide more general international education, orienting all students to the changing world, and not just train a core of specialists. There will be more demand for courses that deal with business and economic questions in all world regions, as well as new approaches to the study of ethnicity and religion. Demands for language skills will both increase and change in nature as more people seek practical and applied language capacities. Courses on world regions and global issues will continue to be important, but some will have to be tailored to fit into the curricula of the professional schools of business, law, public policy, engineering, and the health sciences. We will need to develop new kinds of overseas experiences to meet the needs of a growing and different student body, finding ways other than the traditional semester or college year abroad to develop global competence. Internships, short-term overseas modules, and similar innovative overseas experiences will be needed. These changes will help us develop capstone experiences and credentials that will facilitate entry into new as well as traditional international careers while preparing the general public for life in a more interdependent world.

Other areas of change include devoting more attention to student information and advising. The larger the student body involved in international studies, the more we will encounter students with little or no prior international background. And the more options for international learning we offer, the more complex the choices facing students become. For these reasons, international educators in the future will need to provide more and better information about students' options and strengthen advising services in general.

Finally, we will need to make changes in programs for graduate students. While we need to preserve the strong Ph.D. capabilities that are vital to the production and dissemination of cutting-edge knowledge, we also have to recognize that the demand for Ph.D.s in international studies is flat at best in this country. So we need to explore other kinds of graduate training, including terminal master's degrees with career potential and degrees offered jointly in international studies and professional schools, e.g., a JD/MA in international affairs.

Rethinking Boundaries

The next thing we need to do is to rethink many of the boundaries that were built into our imagination of the international educational complexes and that have shaped the construction of international programs. The current architecture of international education rests on a series of explicit or implicit distinctions and boundaries that need to be rethought. These include boundaries within the international complexes themselves, as well as between the complexes and other entities.

Within the international complex. Intellectually, we have tended to separate the national sphere from the international system of relations among nation-states. And we have separated the public and the private. As a result, international policy studies tend to look either at the national or the interstate level (or both) but often have left the role of corporations, civil society, religious life, and similar matters to be studied elsewhere, if at all. Yet issues like ethnic and religious conflict or the operation and regulation of global financial markets engage public and private actors at multiple levels. In an era when many issues transcend nations and even regions, when the public and private intersect increasingly, and when policies may involve public and private actors at local, national, regional, and global levels, all these boundaries must be rethought.

The same can be said for boundaries that define the scope and limit of interdisciplinary programs on our campuses. We need to rethink both the formal and informal boundaries that have grown up among the elements of the international education complex. Historically, international education in the liberal arts has been separate from studies of international business, law, agriculture and other professional subjects. There has been a tendency for graduate studies to remain separate from undergraduate programs. Even when programs formally served both undergraduate and graduate students, they sometimes drifted toward a focus on the graduate level. Topical programs in fields like arms control or development often were only weakly linked to area studies. In some cases the separate centers for study of individual world regions had little contact with each other, so that specialists on Southeast Asia had only limited interaction with those who studied East Asia, let alone with those who worked on Russia and Europe.

At the UW–Madison, we have recognized the need to bridge many of these gaps. We have brought all our area and international studies programs together into one International Institute. We have created global studies programs that both deal with comparative cultures, global topics, and cross-regional issues and that straddle the public/private divide. We have created a special initiative that brings scholars from economics, political science, sociology, business, law, and other fields together to study new issues relating to the management of the global economy. And new initiatives focus more attention on undergraduates: a new certificate in global cultures; internationally-oriented residential learning on campus; a revitalized undergraduate major in international studies; and a program to support new and innovative types of overseas learning experiences.

Between the international complex and the rest of the university. Another set of boundaries that must be rethought are those between the international education complexes and the rest of the university. These include boundaries between international studies and the departments and colleges, as well as boundaries between the interdisciplinary international studies programs and other parts of the interdisciplinary axis itself. We need a way to reestablish the sense that international studies are central to the concerns of departments like sociology, political science, and economics; we must renew the belief in the interdependence of knowledge in the social disciplines. We also need to break down the barriers between international studies in the liberal arts departments and those in the professional schools of law, business, agriculture, engineering, education, and public policy. At the same time we need to forge relationships with groups pursuing such interdisciplinary topics as ethnic studies, women's studies, environmental studies, and cultural studies.

Between "our" knowledge and "their" knowledge. Another boundary that must be crossed is that between knowledge produced in the United States and knowledge produced in the regions we study. In the past, area studies in the United States seemed to be a project reserved for Americans and carried out primarily on U.S. campuses with occasional forays to "the field." We would send people out to study "the other," and then transmit the learning developed by these American area specialists to our students. To some extent, this practice was a natural response to objective conditions. In some parts of the world there were no local scholars to work with. In others access to local scholars was cut off. In some parts of the world universities were weak or nonexistent, and the only source of scholarly insight on many parts of the world came from scholars in Western universities. The Cold War meant that U.S. researchers were denied access to many countries and contacts with local academics were limited and tightly controlled. Now, however, as a result of decolonialization, economic development, the strengthening of universities around the world, the end of the Cold War, and the global communication revolution, this is no longer the case. Today it is possible for researchers in this country to work closely with counterparts in most countries around the world.

Wisconsin and its sister research universities are responding to these needs by forming closer ties with universities and research centers around the world and by encouraging our faculty to join with peers in "global research networks" that address broad and widely-shared issues like nationalism and ethnic conflict, the globalization of the media, and the changing role of government in the economy. These networks do not privilege any one center of scholarship but seek to work collaboratively on a global basis. In many cases they are virtual networks that operate primarily through the Internet.

Creating New Partnerships

In addition to challenging and transgressing boundaries, progressive international educators are seeking to develop new partnerships and alliances that will sustain and enrich international studies and programs. These include new partnerships on our own campuses as well as partnerships with other universities in the U.S., with universities overseas, and with the public and private sectors. These alliances form part of the basic architecture of the emerging vision of international education.

Within the interdisciplinary axis. The first set of partnerships are those within the interdisciplinary axis of our own universities.

International studies were one of the first elements of the inter-disciplinary axis to be institutionalized. They have been followed by many other cross-departmental and cross-college programs. Among them are programs that study specific ethnic groups in this country (e.g., Afro-American studies, Asian-American stud-ies, and Chicano studies), women's studies, environmental stud-ies, and cultural studies. In each case there are natural affinities between these newer members of the interdisciplinary axis and the international studies complexes. Ethnic studies programs look at populations with roots elsewhere in the word and need to understand from whence these communities have come as well as how they have evolved in the United States. Women's studies pro-grams benefit from comparative knowledge of women's roles and conditions around the world as well as from an understanding of transnational advocacy for and international protection of women. Environmental studies programs similarly require knowl-edge of conditions in other countries and the international arena. And cultural studies is emerging as a global enterprise with inter-ests in the relationship between culture and society worldwide.

While some partnerships have been formed, alliances of this nature have proven more difficult than might be expected. To be sure, some centers of Latin American studies maintain close rela-tions with Chicano studies programs, and some African studies centers work closely with Afro-American studies. But collabora-tions of this nature are not yet commonplace. The reasons are complex. Some programs may be too busy struggling for survival. Others may be concerned about their relations with departments and disciplines and fearful of too much contact with other inter-disciplinary programs that might be looked down on by those wedded to traditional disciplines. At the UW–Madison we have sought to overcome these barriers through joint programs spon-sored by the International Institute and units like the Humanities Institute and the Women's Studies Research Center as well as through a growing number of workshops and other activities put on jointly by area and ethnic studies centers.

With disciplines, departments, and professional fields. The second set of alliances are those between the international education complexes and the units that make up the traditional axis of campus organization. Here there is a need both to redefine old relationships and forge new ones. Traditionally, the international complexes have been closely tied to departments of humanities and social science. Some of these relationships have become frayed in recent years, as new trends within the disciplines have challenged extant approaches to international knowledge and pressures to downsize departments have reopened questions about the role and importance of international knowledge within the disciplines. Efforts are being made to clarify and, if necessary, to redefine these traditional relationships. Area and international studies scholars have tried to forge relationships in two ways: by demonstrating that the social sciences have a need for the insights comparative study can produce, and by refining their scholarship to make it more theoretical and employing the latest empirical techniques. At the same time, they are trying to revive older traditions that stressed the interdependence of the social disciplines and counteract what seems to be "go it alone" tendencies in fields like economics, sociology, and political science. At the UW–Madison we have encouraged intellectual innovation and worked closely with leaders of colleges and departments to ensure that the core area and international studies resources embedded in these units are preserved in times of austerity.

Similar issues arise in the relationship with the humanities as cultural studies and post-colonialism become more important in the humanities and require a redefinition of the relationship between area studies and humanities departments. These newer traditions tend to challenge some of the work that has been done by area scholars in U.S. universities. There is a growing critique of "orientalism" or the tendency to construct knowledge of other societies based on assumptions of Western supremacy. This has led to calls to pay closer attention to, and work more in tandem with, scholars from outside American and Western academic traditions. Area studies centers have to deal with these challenges and incorporate these insights or risk appearing insensitive to the critique of "orientalism." On our campus, we are responding to these challenges by creating joint area programs with universities in the regions we study and by fostering global research networks on topics like democratization, ethnic conflict, and the impact of globalization on labor.

Finally, new relationships are needed with language departments as changes in the constituency for international education creates pressures for new kinds of language instruction. The spread of international education into professional schools and the heightening of career concerns among liberal arts students have generated a need for more intensive and more pragmatic forms of language instruction—hence the rise of courses in Business French, Technical Japanese, and similar forms of "applied" language instruction. At the same time, budgetary pressures are putting some of the less commonly-taught languages at risk. These languages are often essential for the maintenance of area studies capacities, yet the number of students prepared to enroll in languages like Yoruba, Telegu, Thai, Kazakh, or Quechua (all of which are regularly offered at the UW–Madison) are often too small to justify full-time faculty positions in a time of austerity and downsizing. To meet this challenge, the area studies centers and the language departments need to work together in new ways, and language faculty need to take advantage of new technologies to lower the cost of instruction and increase productivity. The UW–Madison, which offers more of these "less commonly-taught" languages than most universities in this country, has taken the lead in developing new methods and building consortia with other universities to support innovation and resource sharing in language instruction.

In addition to redefining traditional alliances, international educators are forging new alliances with departments and colleges that reflect changing conditions and the demands of new constituencies. Perhaps the most important of these are the alliances that are growing up between the liberal arts-based international programs and the professional schools of law, business, agriculture, education, and engineering. Largely as a result of economic globalization, the professional schools at all our research universities have recognized the need to expand their international offerings at all levels. We see this in dramatic form at the UW–Madison. Several of our professional schools have created new international degrees or similar specialized programs and have hired additional international specialists. At the same time, they have sought closer relations with the existing area and international studies programs and asked them to provide specialized training for professional students who want to develop language skills, general area knowledge, and competence on selected global issues. This has led some of the area and international studies programs to revise their curricula and develop specialized offerings more suited to the needs of professional school students. These developments have been supported and encouraged by a special initiative on World Affairs and the Global Economy which brings faculty from the liberal arts and the professional schools together in a cross-campus learning community dealing with problems of management of the global economy.

With other universities. In addition to partnerships on campus, international educators are expanding existing ties and forging new relationships with other universities in the United States and overseas. Faced with increasing demands for international knowledge, and often for knowledge of a novel, complex, and specialized nature at a time when resources are shrinking, university leaders have looked for ways to share resources and cooperate more fully. Thus we increasingly see the development of consortia that link two or more universities for all kinds of specialized tasks. These include jointly-run area studies centers and overseas programs as well as joint programs for research and graduate training on specialized issues. Consortia are also emerging to facilitate the teaching of less commonly-taught languages like

Thai, Kazach, Quechua, or Telegu through summer institutes and distance education. And we are seeking new and deeper relations with individual scholars and research institutions in other countries while also developing global research networks that link our scholars with peers around the world working on similar topics. In the Midwest, the eleven Big Ten universities plus the University of Chicago have worked together in many areas for decades, but only recently have they started to explore cooperation in international studies. In addition to participating in this general consortium, the UW–Madison belongs to many consortia for study abroad, several designed to foster teaching of less commonly-taught languages, and some in area and global studies. Recently, we have created a Joint Center for International Studies with the UW–Milwaukee better to serve the UW System and the state. With the University of Minnesota, we jointly manage the Midwest Center for German and European Studies and with Minnesota and Stanford the MacArthur Consortium on International Peace and Cooperation.

While we are working more closely with sister universities in the United States, we are expanding and deepening our relations with scholars and universities overseas. In particular, we have developed a wide range of partnerships to foster exchange of students and faculty and conduct joint research. This is an area that has been materially helped by U.S. government programs, and thus it is one that is at risk as international education budgets in Washington are cut. Given the nature of these relationships, it will be hard to find alternative sources of support should these cuts be deep and permanent.

With external constituencies. Finally, we are strengthening and deepening relationships with existing constituencies outside the university and trying to build new external alliances. International educators in the research universities have lobbied heavily to preserve existing federal programs that are at risk. We have continued our relationships with the K–12 systems and colleges in our states and regions. Many of us are trying to develop relations with the alumni of our programs as well as with alumni of our universities who reside abroad. In recent years, most universities have sought to strengthen relations with the business community. And many state universities like the UW–Madison have sought a much closer partnership with state government, primarily through alliances with state export promotion offices.

The emerging partnership between state business, state export promotion offices, and state universities is the newest and most innovative of the new external alliances being forged in this time of change. As the economies of states as well as whole regions (like the Midwest) become more and more dependent on exports, business and political leaders have seen the need for more international expertise. In some cases, they have turned to the universities to supply the needed knowledge and training. It is too soon to say if this new alliance will prove mutually beneficial and help take up the slack created by the decline in federal support. But it remains a promising area for future exploration. In the past few years the UW–Madison has developed close relations with the State Department of Commerce and the business community. We have offered a pilot program of workshops, conferences, and other programs on international issues relevant to the state's export promotion program and hope to secure long-term funding to continue these activities.

Preserve Knowledge and Develop New Ideas

The most important of all challenges is the need to preserve the great learning of the past and at the same time develop new concepts and ideas to equip students and others to confront a new world. This is, after all, the central responsibility of research universities in all fields. In our domain, we need to use old and new methods to ensure that our students understand other cultures and societies; to refine our understandings of how world society operates in light of recent trends; to seek new insights about, and appreciation of, the great civilizations of the past; to develop new models of an increasingly globalized world economy; to rethink the interdependence of nations and devise new modalities of governance; to listen to new voices in art and literature from around the world; and to otherwise maintain the highest level of excellence in our scholarship and teaching.

Some Recent Breakthroughs

Over the past decade, a new vision of international education has begun to take shape on our campuses. Emerging out of heated debate and no small amount of struggle, this vision is beginning to shape developments here and elsewhere. As a result, we can point to a number of recent breakthroughs on our campus. Thus, for the first time ever, hiring decisions for a cluster of related faculty in several UW departments have been authorized, and this "cluster hiring" plan has been applied to internationalize policy studies. This reflects campus recognition that the interdisciplinary axis needs the same control over hiring that was once the exclusive preserve of departments, as well as a realization that policy studies in the future must be international. The College of Letters and Sciences and College of Agriculture and Life Sciences have joined with the Schools of Business and Law to create a cross-college learning community on the global economy, thus showing they understand that no single college can create needed knowledge in this area on its own. We have joined with universities in Latin America, Asia, and Africa to create a global research network to study the legacies of authoritarian regimes in politics, culture, and individual psyches, showing that our faculty has seen the need to work with colleagues throughout the world. And member programs of the International Institute have started working together on shared projects, demonstrating that they have recognized that the era of splendid isolation is over.

Conclusion

No one can predict what international education will look like on our campus twenty-five or fifty years from now when the UW–Madison celebrates its next major milestones. International studies, like all higher education, is in flux. But the future is hopeful. The structures of international education in this country have been built on five pillars: strong intellectual interest in the disciplines for matters international; support from top campus leadership; creative work and sustained energy among the international educators; mutually supportive relations between the traditional and the interdisciplinary axes; and strong external support for international higher education. On our campus, these pillars remain strong. As a result, the UW–Madison is increasingly recognized as a leader in international education in our region and nationwide. We have confronted the issues of our times and emerged stronger than ever.

Public Access to University Expertise

Donald A. Nichols

THE PUBLIC'S DEMAND for advanced expertise is growing. Because the research university is the dominant source of such expertise, it is natural to expect that universities would grow to meet the demand. But new organizational forms are springing up to compete with universities as sources of advanced expertise. Perhaps this competition should be expected in a world in which the private sector's dominance over the public sector is growing. And perhaps it should be expected that alternative sources of expertise would arise to serve the many new niches that will develop in an economy of increasingly sophisticated products with an increasingly specialized and professional work force. Since competition from the private sector can be expected to be most intense for the services that are the most lucrative, universities need to be wary of a future in which they are expected to provide only those services that cannot meet a market test, and to fund those services from a shrinking share of an already shrinking public pie.

In this chapter I consider two different markets for expertise, both of which are growing rapidly. One is the provision of expertise to advanced professionals who seek to enhance their careers. The other is the provision of expertise to organizations that seek to enhance their efficiency or profitability. Both of these markets

Donald A. Nichols is professor of economics and public affairs, and director of the Center for World Affairs and Global Economy at the University of Wisconsin–Madison.

provide opportunities for universities to diversify their sources of support and to reduce their dependence on public funding. But while universities are highly competitive, both in their internal organization and in their relations with each other, they are not well-suited to an all out competition with private firms for the most lucrative parts of these two markets.

Universities evolved into their present form in a much different, though equally competitive, environment—one characterized by big science, funded by the federal government, with much of the research intended to meet Cold War needs. The universities that are considered to be the best today are those that met that competition by modifying their internal practices to enhance their competitiveness, while at the same time protecting their core values. The decision to accept large amounts of federal support was awkward for universities at the time, not only because it meant shared control with the federal government over the scientific research agenda, but also because it greatly changed the relative strength and sizes of departments within the university.

These changes were accepted more naturally in the large public research universities with their strong traditions of public service. In particular, the strategy toward federal funding adopted by the University of Wisconsin a half-century ago turned out to be the winning strategy. From the perspective of a scholar at the University of Wisconsin today, the decision to accept large amounts of federal funding seems like an easy choice. Indeed, at UW–Madison it would be rare to hear criticism of scholars who allow their research agendas to be influenced by the availability of federal funding. More typically, success in securing such funding is viewed as a sign of professional distinction.

But a new competition is developing that will require an equally large shift in values for those universities that are to succeed. And while UW–Madison was well placed to succeed in the competition for federal funding over the last fifty years, we are not well placed to succeed in the competition for private funding in the next fifty years. In this competition success is likely to go to universities with strong ties to the private sector and with an ability to accept new forms of relationships between university faculty and private individuals and organizations and to modify those relationships quickly. UW–Madison's strengths in such a competition, in addition to the obvious advantage of starting with an enormous base of expertise, will be its strong alumni. Its disadvantages will be its distance from a large advanced metropolitan area, its distance from a group of large firms that are technologically advanced, and an internal culture of public service that is suspicious of cozy relations with the private sector. Private universities may be more flexible in the kinds of relations with the private sector that they will accept and this outlook may give them an advantage in the competition for private funding.

I am not pessimistic about the future of federal funding. The public is in awe of advanced bio-medical technology and there is continuing pressure in Congress to provide more of it. I believe that the federal government is likely to continue to fund advanced research, especially in biology, where the UW–Madison has expertise that is both broad and deep. Hence, I believe it is possible for UW–Madison to remain a highly-ranked university by continuing to do well in the future what it does so well now. But the most rapidly growing source of demand for advanced expertise is likely to be in the private sector. It is not obvious which universities will be best at meeting this demand, or indeed if universities as a group will remain the dominant source of expertise of commercial value despite the enormous advantage they have today in the expertise they already possess. But we must be alert to the fact that in this competition, UW–Madison will be fighting uphill rather than downhill as it was in the competition for federal funding, because federal funding could be viewed within the university as public service.

The increase in the private demand for expertise will be diffuse. It will vary by industry, occupation, and field, and effective responses to it from the university may have to be decentralized to the departmental or even individual level. Some of the demand will be for proprietary information. Different universities will respond to these opportunities in different ways. Each will seek a balance between the protection of core university values and the recognition that those values must be funded either from support provided at the ballot box or in the marketplace. A new ranking of universities may well emerge out of the new competition, as those who are best at meeting the increased opportunities for private funding while still protecting their core values will find ways to use their new funds to enhance their overall academic quality.

The Evolution of the Research University

The modern research university evolved to its present form through a competitive evolutionary process by providing the best answers to a series of questions of how to organize, develop, and satisfy society's growing need for scientific and professional expertise. To see how universities might fare as sources of expertise in the future, it is necessary first to understand the strengths of the university and how these have been forged in the evolutionary struggles of the past.

Organizations evolve in response to new challenges and opportunities. In competitive American society, the process of evolution is Darwinian, and I will describe the strengths of the modern research university through the Darwinian lens. I will determine whether universities can continue to rely on their past strengths to maintain their position of dominance in the provision of expertise in the future, and how the competition for dominance is likely to play out.

Other kinds of organizations have provided expertise in the past and continue to provide expertise today. Had these competing organizational forms demonstrated a superior ability to develop that expertise or to bring it to the public in the past, they would probably be a much larger source of expertise today. Indeed, even within academia, organizational forms other than research universities have existed in the past and continue to exist today, and any of these could have become the dominant source of expertise had it provided a superior ability to attract and mobilize that expertise in the past.

In this chapter I point out some features of the research university that I feel have helped it become the dominant source of expertise today. I then try to foresee how society's needs for expertise will be met in the future, and in particular whether the research university will continue to play the dominant role in the provision of expertise for public purposes. After describing a few of the features that will affect the Darwinian struggle for survival in the future, I turn to the ways in which the direct provision of expert advice to government, business, and households is likely to change.

Economies of Large Scale in the University

A great strength of American research universities is the synergy that exists among and within the university's three major missions. Research, education, and the direct provision of expertise for other public purposes are complementary missions. Moreover, within each of these missions there are economies of large scale that permit a large organization to do the same task as a smaller organization but at a lower cost, or alternatively, that permit a large organization to do a task of given cost better than a smaller organization. I claim that the organizational form of the modern research university has evolved to take advantage of the synergy provided by those complementarities and economies of large scale.

I will discuss the synergy across missions below. First I will note the existence of economies of large scale within the teaching and research missions. While economies of scale are difficult to document for products that are not sold in a competitive marketplace, a few examples indicate the advantages conveyed by size. UW has the expertise to teach over sixty languages, (though at any given time only forty may be offered.) The curriculum of a university one-tenth the size would differ from this not simply by offering one-tenth as many sections of each of the sixty languages, but the smaller university would be forced to offer far fewer languages because its smaller faculty could not possibly have the necessary expertise to teach sixty languages.

For the same reason, within each language or department, the variety of advanced courses that provide specific forms of expertise can be much greater at a large institution than at a small institution. This is because as universities increase in size, they tend not simply to replicate their existing faculty and curriculum several times over, but instead they tend to hire new kinds of specialists and to offer many more highly specialized courses at the advanced level. This creates additional possibilities for students to develop their special interests. As a result, courses that would suffer from minuscule enrollment at a small university—and therefore be vulnerable as uneconomic—can gain sufficient enrollment at a large university to justify their existence.

The economies of scale are especially evident in research. Every academic department knows how it could increase its quality if it could increase the number of its faculty doing research, even if the average quality of the faculty being added is no greater than the quality of the existing faculty. The possibility of covering additional specialties adds to the collective strength of the department. Problems that have been conquered in one specialty tend to reappear in other specialties, and the larger the faculty the more likely it is that one's colleagues can provide advice that is helpful in moving one's research along. National networks link the best experts across the country—indeed the world—together. If one's colleagues are numerous and of high quality, they will be in these networks and they can be very helpful in providing access to people who can help or even collaborate on research. The more colleagues one has, the more access one has to these national networks. And even when strength in a given specialty is duplicated with large size, the ability to renew a field more frequently by the accelerated addition of younger colleagues improves a field's average quality.

Of fundamental importance to how a university can to maintain its quality is its ability to make personnel decisions accurately and confidently. The faculty in a department of large size can assess the quality of its potential future members with a high degree of accuracy. Because they must do this frequently, they get good at the process and become confident in their judgments. Hence this decision can be left to the faculty in large departments at a good research university. Smaller departments will have faculty in only a few fields, and while they may be able to assess the work of others in their own specific fields, they are less confident about the quality of people in areas a bit removed from their own specializations or less confident in their ability to judge the need to appoint people with those specialties. Moreover, the infrequency with which they must make decisions over promotion, for example, make them quite uncomfortable with the process.

Even outside the department, but still within the research mission, there are economies of scale. Because the interests of faculty and advanced students overlap across departments, a strong economics department is easier to maintain in a university with strong statistics, mathematics, computer science, finance, and operations research departments. Similarly a strong economics department makes it easier to maintain strong departments in a variety of other social science disciplines.

In research, bigger is better. I qualify that statement by noting that when I say that bigger is better, I say it with the unspoken assumption of *ceteris paribus* that is implicit in many of the broad statements economists make. In research, bigger is better, other things being equal. And the good research universities are big, at least in comparison to other institutions of higher learning today and in comparison to the size of universities in times past.

University Culture #1: The Pursuit of Excellence

The usefulness of one's colleagues to one's own research was noted above. Here the same point is used as the motivation for the pursuit of excellence within departments. The stronger one's colleagues are, the easier it is for one to remain abreast of developments in one's field. The interests of faculty overlap. The people in my department whose work is closest to my own can provide useful advice to me on how to solve problems I might face. They can attract faculty from other universities to come and give useful seminars that will help me keep up. They will attract good students to do graduate work under them—students who will help my own students keep up with the latest developments in peripheral fields. This means that the students I can employ as research assistants to move my own work along will be better if my colleagues are better. Hence I have a strong incentive to appoint the best colleagues I can find.

This force is so strong that it goes a long way by itself toward explaining why great faculty tend to gravitate toward each other, and hence to collect in a small number of institutions. The better one's colleagues are, the better one can be.

Institutions whose faculty are driven by the pursuit of excellence in their own work will tend to demand excellence from their colleagues. And if they demand excellence in their colleagues and they act upon that excellence when making personnel decisions, there will be a tendency for the highest quality faculty to gravitate together. If the faculty are free to move, they will do so and large groupings of excellent faculty will emerge. In a Darwinian world, these groupings will have the ability to maintain their excellence in a competition with other groupings. Hence, the system of excellence is self-sustaining, and the relative rankings of universities are quite stable.

University Culture #2: Competition as the Driving Force

The driving force that permits a set of excellent faculty to group together is an intertwined set of competitions within each of the major groupings of students, faculty, and universities. Universities are meritocracies. Students compete to get into the best universities. Faculty compete to be the best in their fields, which leads them to seek appointments at universities that have other outstanding faculty. Finally, universities compete to attract the best students and faculty.

Out of this competition comes a well-defined hierarchy of research universities in which the best universities end up having the best students and the best faculty. The best faculty are needed to attract the next generation of great faculty and to make the shrewd decisions about who those faculty members will be. The universities compete to attract those professors, and they do so by providing the best working conditions, which means the best environment for research, so that the faculty can reach their potential. The universities also provide an environment in which the pursuit of excellence is visible as the primary value that will govern all major academic decisions. Faculty will trust the steadfastness of institutions that have a long tradition of honoring this value. A university that falls behind on this front is unlikely to maintain its greatness for long.

The competition among faculty, students, and universities creates and sustains a hierarchy of institutional quality that is so robust that it changes little from generation to generation. These competitions interact. The best students seem to be attracted to the best research universities, which after all are only a small fraction of the institutions of higher learning, most of which emphasize teaching, not research. While each individual student may not be aware of the driving role played by research in maintaining the quality of the institutions that are most in demand by other students, the continued success of students who have chosen a particular set of universities is unlikely to be random, and can be used as a reliable indicator of the soundness of the decision to choose to matriculate at any particular institution. The result is that the twenty or thirty major research universities—universities whose research budgets rival their teaching budgets—are the most sought after by students.

After matriculation at a research university, students find themselves in a continuing competition with other top students, and they find themselves in classes led by faculty with inquiring minds. These faculty are extremely bright, which is a necessity if the minds of the brightest students are to be sharpened, and they approach questions that arise in class as researchers. That is, by being researchers, they answer questions in a style that teaches students to have inquiring minds. The best answers to the deeper questions are typically not of the mode "Where can we look that up?" but, "How should I think about this question and how can I create an answer to it?" Responses in this mode are instinctive to researchers, and students whose minds have been sharpened in classes led by researchers learn not only a list of known answers to known questions, but also how to think about new problems and how to ask and answer questions on their own.

University Culture #3:
Integrity and the Pursuit of Knowledge

The pursuit of knowledge is the overriding value that governs individual behavior in universities. Absolute integrity on the part of each individual faculty member, student, and administrator is required if this system is to function properly. In particular, the assessment of the quality of new knowledge and of the level of professional attainment of individuals must be done in an absolutely objective fashion if the university system is to function. The importance of the objective reporting of one's own work and of the links of that work to the work of others is unquestioned.

Cultures find ways of institutionalizing their values to strengthen them. Values become codified into norms of behavior for individual members and, in universities, for departments to follow. Within the university a governance structure has been created to see that the primacy of academic values is maintained against forces from without—such as changes in political fashions or in opportunities for financial gain—that might provide strong incentives for individual faculty or departments to modify their behaviors. The governance structure penalizes deviation from academic values and it rewards behavior that conforms to the accepted norms.

Given the integrity in the evaluation of individuals and ideas (including one's own), universities have reached their present form through a culture of competition and excellence in the pursuit of knowledge. The governance structure among faculty serves to perpetuate that culture and to strengthen its influence.

Evolution and Change in American Universities

Evolution involves competition both within and across species. I have identified the nature of competition that goes on within and among universities. To ask how universities might evolve in the future, it is also useful to take a brief look at how they have evolved in the past. The objective is to gain insight into the kind of competition universities might face in the future, particularly in their efforts to provide expert advice to private business.

Many of the private institutions that began the twentieth century as strong research universities had begun the nineteenth century as small colleges with classical curricula. At the start of the nineteenth century, most of the students in these institutions were trained for the ministry. Latin, Greek, and Hebrew, along with philosophy and theology, were the required disciplines. Science departments were small and mixed in quality, with scientists holding formal appointments in the philosophy department.

Boyer (1990) notes that when Jefferson sent Lewis and Clark westward in 1803, he chose Lewis from a position in government service and he trained him in science not by sending him to a university, but by sending him to Philadelphia to study with members of the American Philosophical Society. By the end of the nineteenth century, science departments were well established at the major universities, and the selection of faculty members in the sciences was based largely on the criterion of research excellence, as it is today.

During the course of the nineteenth century, university curricula were modified for many reasons, including the demands of students for practical knowledge. In the elite privates, the demands came from students who were the sons of rich southern planters and of rich northern bankers and merchants. These students wanted a curriculum that would prepare them for leadership. On their own, the students organized debating clubs, newspapers, literary societies, and other activities into which they devoted the bulk of their energies. Meanwhile gentleman's Cs were earned by these students in a curriculum that they viewed as irrelevant—mostly courses in Latin, Greek, and religion—and the faculty in these required classes were scorned, as were the poor, more conscientious students who were training to be ministers, and who took these classes seriously.

Meanwhile in the West, the Northwest Ordinance of 1787 had provided grants of land for universities to be established in each of the states in the Northwest territories. These universities were expected to provide practical training in the professions needed to organize a modern society. The Morrill Act of 1862 and the Hatch Act of 1887 offered even more land to universities in exchange for even more specific requirements that universities were to provide training in the practical arts and to make their expertise available to the private sector. By the end of the century these new universities had established colleges of agriculture, law, engineering, medicine, and education in addition to the core college of the liberal arts, which remained the sole college in many of the smaller private institutions.

Given the substantial advantage of public funding, the new public universities were able to compete for the best faculty not only with each other but also with the private universities. Competition was carried out not only in the form of the payment of competitive salaries but also in the manner described above, which was to provide the resources and necessary environment for the faculty member to pursue an active program of research. Whether public or private, once a university's reputation as a great research university was secured, it was very difficult for competing organizations to dislodge it.

In the twentieth century, the evolutionary challenges were challenges of opportunity, not survival. The number of students seeking a university education grew enormously. This was fed by the demand of an increasingly technical and complicated economy, by an increasing democratization of society, and by large increases in governmental funding, largely at the state level, but including, most notably, the GI Bill at the federal level. The valuable role played by scientists in World War II, including the dramatic demonstration of the power of science in the atomic bomb, led to increased federal funding for science, not only for Cold War technology but also for health and agriculture.

The increased funding for research played to the strength of the great public universities and their research budgets grew enormously. At the same time, the pool of expertise available to meet the needs of external organizations also grew, though the pattern of needs of nonfederal external organizations was quite different from the well-funded needs of the federal government. Of course, by then the liberal arts had changed substantially from the Greek and Latin that had been taught as practical skills to future ministers. In response to the demands for reform of the curriculum in the mid-nineteenth century, the liberal arts now included much larger science departments as well as departments in such fields as English literature, in which writing and other practical skills were taught.

As we look to the future it would seem that the universities are in a very strong position. The age of information is upon us. Universities are the ultimate source of the most complicated information we have. They are the creators of the most fundamental information needed for advances in living standards worldwide, and because of the synergies outlined above, the grouping of many individuals with advanced expertise into faculty clusters of energetic, high quality—even brilliant, individuals at research universities gives the university enormous advantages in maintaining its position for the foreseeable future. Furthermore there is a culture on university campuses based on a set of values that have the support and loyalty of the faculty, and a set of self-governing institutions is in place to nurture, protect, and perpetuate these values.

But the future will bring challenges; meeting these challenges will require change. The brief review of the evolution of the research university can give the mistaken impression that at major turning points in the past, the acceptance of change required no more than the recognition of the new opportunities offered by change. We are the survivors of the evolutionary struggle just described, and in our eyes the universities have attained a perfection that can only be improved upon by a spontaneous change in faculty opinion concerning what organizational form is likely to provide the ideal conditions under which to pursue learning and discovery. Yet viewed from the perspective of contemporaries, each of the major changes the universities have undergone was threatening, and each had losers. If we could return to the year 1850 and describe the modern research university in all its detail to a professor of Greek literature, and then ask his (I can safely say "his") opinion of such a university, he might well sniff at it and view it as a trade school for the commercial classes.

The lesson of history is that change will happen regardless of our opinion of it, and that those universities who win the Darwinian struggle of coming years and who will be ranked at the forefront of universities fifty years from now will be the ones that find a way to meet the challenges along the way, to redesign the way they do business, and to use the opportunities for new resources to strengthen their core.

In my view, a major challenge will come in the form of increased competition from sources of expertise outside the university. Universities will encounter this challenge first in the form of competition for the provision of expertise to the public. It should try to meet this challenge and to learn from the difficulties it encounters in doing so.

The Organizational Challenge

I see three organizational challenges universities must face as they cope with the increased demand for their expertise and as they meet increased competition from other organizations in providing these needs. These challenges arise from the need to mesh the university more closely with outside organizations that are quite different from itself. The challenges involve: (1) a clash of values between the internal and external cultures; (2) a clash of reward systems with widely different internal and external pay premiums for different professional specialties; and (3) a widening external gap between the nature of and the strength of the public and private sectors, both of which have needs for access to university expertise.

The university must strengthen its links both to government and to the private sector and it must do that while maintaining its sustaining internal values and the forms of governance that are a major source of its strength. It must also succeed at this complicated endeavor by being better than government and better than the private sector at what it does, and it must accomplish this in a rapidly changing economic and political environment. Furthermore, it must succeed at this endeavor while being part of the public sector, a sector that is in retreat. The universities that dominate the twenty-first century will be those who successfully meet these challenges and establish themselves as strong participants in the private marketplace for expertise.

Adaptation to the changed environment will be made more difficult for universities by decades of neglect of their public images. The public views research universities as educational institutions and it views the faculty as teachers. When the public thinks of universities, the first image is not of institutions that represent the wellsprings of our advances in living standards and life expectancy or of an understanding of history and foreign cultures reaching levels necessary to sustain world peace. People think of universities as educational institutions where students go to study thirteenth- to sixteenth-grade material. In the past this confusion has not hurt the universities. Indeed, it may even have helped them gain funding. But on the horizon is a vast and sweeping reform of public education at the K–12 levels, and universities could well find themselves included in these reforms in ways that damage the sources of their strength, simply because the role they play in our society is misunderstood.

Providing Expertise to Advanced Professionals

Public demand for university expertise can be divided into two categories: There is a demand by individuals for education and training that can help them develop their professional skills; and there is a demand by organizations for new technologies and increased efficiency through internal reform. I am aware that in many cases organizations demand—and pay for—the training of their employees. But the needs of the individual and the needs of the organization are not the same and are often met in different ways. I am interested here in the changing nature of the demands for advanced expertise by both individuals and organizations.

While the provision of expertise to the public is a mission that universities can easily sustain if they organize themselves to do the job, a problem that universities have always confronted when trying to fulfill this mission is that the mission itself does not seem to strengthen the university the way additional research funding does. That is, the mission of the sharing of expertise seems to be easy, but only because the expertise is already there and because there are so few competing sources of expertise. Faculty members have not naturally gravitated toward this mission, nor has the expansion of this mission strengthened the university's core expertise in the way that an equivalent expansion of funding for its other missions would. It has been the case, however, that the university has gained enormous *political* support for the quality of the outreach it has provided.

Of course, in the past, universities had little competition in fulfilling this mission. This is about to change. Competition has been light because it has been prohibitively expensive for private organizations to build and sustain their own centers of expertise. Because of the enormous synergies involved once a center of expertise has been established in a university, universities have been able to fulfill the outreach mission with their left hands. Furthermore, much past provision of expertise has been funded by government, because the expertise was to be provided to a broad class of individuals seeking entry-level professional skills or even general education at basic levels. Or it was provided to the one industry—agriculture—that was politically favored because it had a large, important class of voters. But this situation has changed as the number of farmers continues to shrink.

In the future, the largest growth in demand is likely to come from high level professionals—past university graduates who seek to keep up with advanced developments in their fields. Some of the demands will be for extremely specific, even factual, training about how to be productive in these advanced fields. This is an area where universities have no natural advantage; indeed they may not even have the expertise needed to provide training of this kind. Because of the increased complexity of modern professions and organizations, the need for these task-specific skills is increasing very rapidly.

Working professionals will have mixed needs that include the specific experiential knowledge of this kind along with the more advanced and abstract knowledge that the universities are best at providing. A challenge for the universities is that the professionals who demand this advanced knowledge may well prefer one-stop shopping. Organizations like Arthur Andersen, who may be the best providers of the experiential training, may find it easy to provide the methodological education as well, simply by hiring university faculty on a consulting basis for a few hit-and-run lectures.

It has been observed that one implication of advances in information and communication technologies has been the development of star systems in many industries. Bob Frank and Phil Cook call this the "Winner Take All Economy." The implication for advanced outreach is that a few faculty, say at the Harvard Business School, will have the ability to reach a wide audience by providing taped lectures in video and audio form. Private consulting firms could provide advanced education to adult students by requiring the students to listen to these lectures on their own—perhaps in their cars—then to appear in person for some intensive drill and analysis with a few extremely engaging local lecturer/consultants, and then to pass the exam "used at Stanford" to acquire advanced certification. University faculty would grade those exams for a certain fee, especially if those faculty had ongoing relationships with the consulting firm.

Partnerships with Professional Associations

Increasingly, the demand by individuals for advanced training may come through their professional organizations; these organizations may play a growing role in determining the nature and level of expertise being sought. Some professions are long established and have strong associations that are closely tied to state regulatory bodies, which enforce members' requirements for continuing advanced training. Other associations are much newer and are loose associations of executives who have been assigned the same technical function by their various employers. These employees simply gather to learn from each other. Closer relations between universities and these professional associations may help bridge the gap from the university to the private sector.

Professional associations have the potential to organize and to provide their own advanced education and training. Consider how the bar association, an organization of a mature profession, provides continuing education for its members. Attorneys must accumulate a specific number of credits per year of continuing legal education in order to remain certified to practice law. The bar association organizes programs that provide these credits. A typical program would rely to a great extent on practicing attorneys as faculty. Judges, public officials and university faculty can also be invited to participate, but the programs are organized and certified by the bar associations, not the law schools. Law schools can organize their own programs and can ask the bar associations to bless these programs by including them in the list of programs that will earn credits, but the decisions over which programs earn credits and which do not lie with the associations, not the law schools.

Professional associations in engineering, journalism, the civil service, and the business professions are less institutionalized for historical reasons, though the potential exists for these associations to take charge of their own executive training in the way the bar associations do. The increasing analytic difficulty of formal training in many of these professions, the increasing complexity and specificity of the functions performed by members of these occupations, and the difficulty of the lay public in determining who is or who is not competent to provide these services are forces that are likely to lead to increased self-regulation, including requirements for organized adult education and training.

Universities are natural sources of expertise to provide some of this training, but they are not the only source. The governing members of these associations often have greater specific knowledge of the needs of the profession and even of the expertise itself than do university faculty. Universities have greater expertise in the more abstract or formal knowledge which is only one of the forms of advanced education that will be in demand.

While partnerships are a natural way for this training to evolve, the university's inclusion in these partnerships is not automatic. Funding for this advanced training typically comes from the participants. While some of the associations have a claim on public support—for example, for the continued training of public school teachers—others do not. Where public support is strong and where it is provided through the universities, university participation can be assumed. But in associations where public support has not played a role, say in the certifying of chartered financial advisors, the association will typically take the lead in organizing the training and the examining, and university faculty participation in the training could be on a variety of different bases, including that of consultants, with fees paid for specific lectures.

Nonuniversity organizations could offer competing programs

for providing and certifying professional expertise. The consulting firm of Arthur Andersen, for example, already provides its own MBA. University faculty may be invited to offer lectures as part of the MBA, but the lecture fees are paid to them as individuals and not to their departments or programs. One could envision a future in which the competition between universities and these private firms would be quite intense, and in which the ability of the private firms to cherry pick the best faculty and to offer only the most lucrative training programs would leave the universities at a great competitive disadvantage.

A final advantage of the universities is that university faculty members are well suited to certify expertise. This is because they possess expertise at the highest level and because they spend much of their lives assessing the work of their students and colleagues. But it is also easy for faculty to do because the ethics that dominate academia require that the identity of the individual being assessed must play no role in the judgment being rendered. Private firms whose purpose is to make money may find it tempting to improve the grades for those participants who have large contracts with them. This force gives universities a natural advantage in the market for certification.

Providing Expertise to Private Organizations

Business firms and other organizations also seek expertise, often to gain a competitive advantage. The difficulties of meshing the incentives of the universities and these private organizations will continue to provide a major challenge to university governance throughout the twenty-first century.

As noted above, the strength of universities rests on a culture of internal values that are expressed through a strongly honed competition for reputation and funding both among individuals and institutions. The free pursuit of knowledge for its own sake and the free provision of all knowledge is bedrock to the university culture. But private firms often need secrecy. Hence, universities will be torn as their internal culture leads them one way while the need to remain competitive will lead another.

The advantage of close links to the private sector is not just that the private sector brings much-needed funding. The private sector also brings to academia very practical and important research problems. While there are advantages in having the agenda for faculty research be set within academia, there are also advantages in having the end users of that research define the agenda. Furthermore, many faculty will derive satisfaction from the knowledge that their work is of immediate practical use, and they will press their universities, both through the internal governance process and through their mobility, to permit relationships with private organizations even if those relationships require compromises with the most rigid interpretations of the university's internal values. A likely result is that the forces of competition both within the university and among universities will lead them to seek ever-closer relationships with particular firms and industries. This would occur not simply because private firms can provide the funding for advanced research, but also because these firms often bring exciting and well-defined research problems that faculty find attractive.

In some cases, faculty who pursue close relations with private business will find it necessary to maintain labs both in the university and in private firms. Advanced students will also have skills that are attractive to the private firms and may be able to finance their graduate training by becoming employees of the private firms while simultaneously working toward their degrees. It is likely that firms who provide a home for faculty research may end up providing education for their students as well. One could imagine that a large firm with a practice of life-time employment could find it profitable to fund its own lab with employees demonstrating the highest level of competence. These employees could simulate the university environment with the internal award of degrees to employees who have met the standard required by universities for equivalent degrees.

The most extreme demonstration of private sector research

accomplishment has led in the past to the Nobel Prize being awarded to employees of both IBM and AT&T. Both of these firms were protected from market competition when the research was done, and as a result they were then able to entice scientists to work for them by promising them the ability to publish their results freely. Employment in more competitive environments is less likely to provide free public access to research results.

The blending of teaching with employment is evident not just at the advanced research level but can be seen across the curriculum. Undergraduates in many fields find it to their advantage to pursue internships with nonuniversity organizations. Even at the undergraduate level the specificity of the tasks to be performed by graduates in entry positions are so refined that only by having held internships prior to graduation are these students ready to be productive employees upon graduation.

Universities may have to support close ties to the private sector if they wish to be ranked highly in the next century. Universities that do not accept, or maybe even pursue, close relationships with the private sector will fall behind in funding and in the retention of those faculty whose professional careers would greatly profit from close relations to business. Yet the universities cannot sacrifice their core values to this competition, because those values are the ultimate source of the strength and vigor of the modern research university. Hence, to be successful in the competition likely to arise among universities in the next fifty years, schools will need to strike the proper balance between these seemingly opposed forces.

The need to strike such a balance is already upon us, and in the struggle to reconcile the internal and external forces, a whole set of institutions has been created to buffer the core of the university from the hurly burly of the marketplace. The search for a workable institutional structure will continue; perhaps many solutions will be required. That is, the different professions and industries may each find that a different institutional solution fits its own needs best. There may be no "one size fits all" answer to this challenge. This means that faculty codes of ethics and university-wide policies toward relations with profit-making firms may need to be continually re-written, amended, and elaborated to meet emerging needs. Part of the competition among universities will be to find such workable institutions quickly.

The University Hospital: The Relationship between the University and the Market

The university hospital provides a well-developed example of the strength of the forces at work when the private market confronts university culture. The hospital is the major institution through which medical expertise is provided by the university to the public. Competition among universities for the best medical research faculty has led universities to accept substantial non-salary compensation for medical doctors employed by universities. At UW–Madison, the recent spinning off of the university hospital from the university was forced by competition in the marketplace for medicine.

An increasingly awkward feature of compensation arrangements like the one successfully in place for medical school faculty is the widening differential that emerges between the rates of compensation in the different fields. This widening differential is a feature not just of closer competition between universities and private business but is a well-known development within the private sector itself in recent years. Compensation of high-level professionals has grown much more rapidly than compensation of nonprofessionals in recent decades.

One view of this widening differential is that it will ultimately redound to the benefit of the university because the value of a university education and of advanced professional training both to individuals and to society have increased. But because universities are publicly funded and because the public views the university as an educational institution and not as a source of expertise, faculty salaries have not kept up with private salaries in many

189

professions. The bulk of the voters and taxpayers are nonprofessional, and they fail to see the need to keep university faculty salaries competitive with private professionals, especially if that seems to require a ratification on their part of a widening private pay differential that they resent. Hence it has been very difficult to marshal political support to improve faculty salaries.

If faculty salaries continue to advance slowly because of a lack of political support, and if private pay differentials between professional and nonprofessional occupations continue to widen, university faculty in highly compensated fields will continue to be drawn to a variety of arrangements that provide compensation in addition to the university salary, as happened with the hospital. These will range from consulting to part-time employment to partial ownership of the outside venture. The nature of the professional involvement will vary from the provision of isolated doses of expertise to upper management or advanced professionals to partnership in long-lasting joint research ventures. In some of these outside ventures, faculty may provide services to organizations that compete with universities.

While large compensation differentials are not intrinsically inconsistent with any fundamental university value, they do arouse resentment and even jealousy, and some extremely persuasive faculty members may channel these natural human feelings into divisive activities.

The La Follette Institute: The Relationship between the University and the Private Sector

The La Follette Institute for Public Affairs trains civil servants and provides expertise to government. The provision of expertise to the public sector is one of the traditional outreach missions of public universities. La Follette fulfills this mission in ways that are both traditional and modern. The faculty of the La Follette Institute are organized into a department in the College of Letters and Science, but there is no undergraduate major in public affairs.

The instructional component of the institute is a professional training program for civil servants at the master's degree level.

Faculty at the institute are drawn from several disciplines, and they carry out individual research programs. While these faculty typically have joint appointments in departments with graduate research programs, the faculty are drawn together by their mutual interest in the problems of public policy and in the methods of public policy research. Their joint knowledge, experience, and professional expertise provides an environment that is collectively attractive for them as experts who wish to do research on issues of public policy, even though the methods they use vary widely, reflecting their diverse backgrounds. By controlling the process through which new members of the faculty are appointed, the existing faculty ensure that future colleagues bring expertise and experience of the kind most likely to enrich the existing environment and to help provide the synergy that makes existing faculty productive and hence that binds them closely to the program. An active seminar series at La Follette provides the faculty with the opportunity to keep abreast of their colleagues' activities and of developments in fields related to their own.

Public policy is becoming increasingly complex. At one time, the public sector's need for expertise was so simple that university professors could fill those needs without devoting their careers to the individual problems under consideration. But the increased specialization that is required to formulate modern social or environmental policy makes it less likely that armchair advice can be useful in the future. The increased need for expertise has led the government to employ internal groups of experts who work on these problems full time. This trend is likely to continue. The use of university expertise is more and more likely to occur only for overall agency guidance, for the certification of the findings of an agency's experts, or for consultative or review panel purposes.

In La Follette, individual faculty have strong decentralized links to different parts of state government. They provide expertise in a wide variety of ways. While La Follette provides an excellent example of how the university continues to meet one of the traditional missions of public service, namely that of providing expertise to the public sector, the lesson in this example for the twenty-first century is the diversity of the ways in which the expertise of the La Follette faculty finds its way to the public.

Decentralization of decision making is a feature that is becoming more common in large organizations. The advantage of decentralization is the ability to tailor the manner in which the expertise is provided to the clients' needs. The disadvantage is the difficulty of enforcing a common set of procedures to govern such relationships—procedures which take on great importance where relationships between the university and the private sector are concerned.

Many La Follette faculty provide expertise to government and public purpose agencies. The institute supports outreach with funding and a professional support staff. However, there is no single organizational model to describe the way in which La Follette reaches out to the public. The links between the faculty and the public agencies vary widely by agency and faculty member. The institute's activities over the last few years reflect how it provides expertise in many ways.

La Follette faculty have helped reform public sector agencies and programs at both the state and local level. Some faculty have had close involvement in the design of the new Wisconsin welfare program and will continue to work closely with the state agency that administers the program. A major conference organized by students was held in 1998 to evaluate the experience of Project New Hope, a three-year demonstration of the effect of increasing the opportunities for employing hard-to-employ residents of some selected Milwaukee neighborhoods. The small, experimental school choice program was and continues to be evaluated by a La Follette faculty member.

The Campaign Finance Reform Commission was headed by Donald Kettl, a La Follette faculty member. Kettl also served on the SAVE Commission, helping the commission to direct itself.

192

Staff for the commission came from La Follette, including members who edited the final *Commission Report*. I recently served on the Governor's Export Strategy Commission. Over the years, many La Follette faculty have testified before a wide variety of commissions and public hearings.

The La Follette Center for State, Local and Tribal Governance sponsored numerous speakers and training for town and village officials, city mayors, tribal nations, and others on issues ranging from performance budgeting to evaluation skills. The institute helped the Department of Natural Resources by evaluating major new environmental management systems; cosponsoring, with the DNR and the Wharton School of Business, a national meeting on ISO14000; and contracting with the EPA to explore barriers to innovative technology in the pulp and paper industry.

Michael Wiseman, the course instructor of the basic policy methods course, recently required that his students complete a project working in conjunction with the Milwaukee mayor's office. The class helped Milwaukee officials analyze data and policy on topics including the state's spending cap, police squad vehicle replacement, brownfield redevelopment, civil service reform, school construction proposals, voter registration, and more. The results of these student projects have helped city government reform itself.

Conferences have been held to help communities form a strategy toward violence in gangs of youths. More than a dozen Wisconsin communities have come through this program, which includes research, outreach, and discussion to approach youth violence and gangs as a public health issue that has reached epidemic proportions. This unique model includes bringing together a community team of business owners, church officials, education professionals, nonprofit leaders, youth, law enforcement officers, and others to develop novel strategies based on new ways to coordinate the provision of services to the public.

The Bowhay Institute for Legislative Leadership Development funds training programs for new legislators with leadership potential. For the last four years, the Midwest Office of the Council of State Governments has chosen La Follette as its partner in offering a week-long training program funded by Bowhay. Over 125 legislators from 12 states have participated in these programs to date.

La Follette is planing a three-day seminar to be held in summer 1998 for the heads of the biggest federal agencies in the Midwest region under the auspices of the Federal Executive Board. More than 50 of the 170 federal agencies with offices in the Chicago area are expected to send their top-level managers to this conference.

La Follette faculty are also called upon to make individual public presentations—to legislators and civil servants—both through the mass media and at meetings of public policy groups. Many La Follette faculty have personal links to state government and to specific members of that government that lead to individual small assignments too numerous for La Follette to catalog. Other contacts include numerous phone calls; occasional participation on a recruiting panel; or sitting on a panel to select a vendor for a state agency research contract or technical service.

Because La Follette studies the public sector and because it provides expertise to the public sector, it often does so with funding provided for that purpose from the university budget. In these cases it does not sell its services and hence does not face competition from the private sector. If the provision of expertise is expected to be temporary or of limited intensity, the public agency would typically not provide compensation. This is usually the case for activities that are provided on a one-time basis, such as a presentation by a faculty member or service by a faculty member on a committee or commission where private citizens serve without compensation.

Private sector experts may also provide free services to government, sometimes of an extensive nature. These services are also funded, at least implicitly, by the expert's employer in a manner that seems to be a parallel to that of the university. But the parallelism is not complete. The private firm helps out on public commissions in part to be a good citizen, in part to influence the outcome, and in part simply to be *viewed* as a good citizen, which is a useful reputation for the future. An extreme example of the self-serving provision of expertise to the public sector is lobbying, which is not the subject here. Lobbyists provide scientific studies that are advantageous to their cause. They may even offer to write legislation. Since they give this advice away free, it is hard for the university to match their price.

The university, on the other hand, provides these services to the public sector as an expected part of its mission. And the faculty who provide these services do so on what appears to them to be an uncompensated basis. Remember that these faculty are also involved in an intense competition for preeminence in research with faculty at competing institutions. And while some direct involvement with the public sector helps the faculty learn about how the world works, each appearance draws them away from their research.

Where more extensive contact is required, or where intensive research is needed to identify the problems, government agencies will often provide a research grant or contract to individual faculty members to study the issue. The results of the project will typically include a published study, often publicized at a conference attended by public officials. In addition, the project generates new expertise, held by the faculty members and the students who conducted the research. This expertise will usually be drawn upon in the future to help with the practical problems of the implementation of the policy.

Private sector firms occasionally compete for these research grants. If the need for research is ongoing, the public agency will create an office that will organize the research process. The agency will acquire its own in house expertise, and these experts can answer the day to day questions that faculty would otherwise be drawn upon to answer.

Access to University Expertise through Captive Nonprofit Organizations

Many universities, including UW–Madison, have created private nonprofit organizations and have assigned to them some of the activities that involve the sale of expertise in competitive markets. The intent is to alleviate some of the internal administrative difficulties that can arise when pursuing both knowledge and profit within the university. A wide range of these organizations has already been created and more are likely to be seen in the future. No single template is likely to be suitable for all situations.

These public-private organizations can be controversial. Because of the difficulties that are inherent in the competing missions of these organizations, it is important for the detractors to remember that their roles are to allow universities to participate in a wider array of activities than would otherwise be possible. Because of synergy and economies of scale within the university, a wider array of activities in which it can compete will ensure, on average, a higher quality of the university in the pursuit of all of its missions, including the creation of knowledge.

UW–Madison, like most large public universities, is already surrounded by a group of supporting nonprofit organizations, some quite old and uncontroversial, that have a mix of public and private motives. Managing these diverse organizations has yielded constructive experience, and that experience should be drawn upon to design new organizations to take advantage of new opportunities in the market for expertise. Examples of organizations at UW–Madison that pursue a public purpose but that finance themselves completely from the sale of private goods and services are the Wisconsin Union, Residence Halls, University Research Park, and the hospital. There are many other supportive organizations that are financed in part, or even largely, by outside funding, including the large Department of Athletics. And finally there are organizations that are directly involved in the marketing of expertise at the most advanced level. These include the Wisconsin Alumni Research Foundation, the Center for University-Industry Relations, and some self-supporting components of the university's traditional outreach efforts, such as the Management Institute.

In my view the university will increasingly need to depend on organizations of this kind as the market for university-level expertise grows. The university should not shrink from this increasing market but should instead view it as an opportunity to broaden its financial base. The university should enter into this market with full awareness that the pursuit of profit and the pursuit of knowledge do not always overlap, but often do. The strongest universities of the future are likely to be the ones who create organizational structures that allow them to capture some of the huge financial returns to expertise and creativity that are available in private markets, but who do it in a manner that protects their core values. An innovative use of captive nonprofit organizations is likely to play a larger role in the competition among universities in the future than it has in the past. If other universities are going to be good at this, UW–Madison will suffer in competition with these new champions if it fails to pursue these opportunities vigorously.

In some circles, UW–Madison is already viewed as the model of how to market university expertise. In other circles, the wide gap between the university's expertise and the needs of state industry are often descried in a negative way. This suggests that we are striking a balance somewhere in the middle. To preserve our strength in the future, we will need to be sure that we continue to strike the right balance.

Conclusion

It is by now a trite observation that we live in the age of information. It seems natural to expect that because the university lies at the core of society's increasingly complicated system of information, that universities will be one of the natural growth industries of the twenty-first century. But other forces may restrain their growth. One major restraint to university growth that emerged in the late twentieth century is that voters seem to have lost faith in the public sector's ability to use tax revenues wisely. The simple fact that many large universities are in the public sector has restrained their growth even as the value of all information and expertise-related functions in the economy has increased, and even as it is recognized that the university lies at the core of these functions.

At one level, expertise is just information, and the ways in which information can be transferred have changed enormously in recent years and will continue to change. At other levels, of course, expertise is much more. Indeed, it takes a lot of expertise just to understand some information. And some forms of expertise are not information at all but rather are ways of thinking about and solving problems. Hence the transfer of complicated information to business and government often involves the training of professionals in business and government who can understand and use the expertise. But even the ways in which these higher levels of expertise are transferred can change substantially; as they change, the overlap of activities that meet one or more of the university's three traditional missions will change as well.

The huge cadres of professionals that were trained by universities in the last fifty years would seem to provide a natural market for university expertise. Furthermore, the need for expertise by government and private organizations will continue to grow beyond the organizations' capacity to provide for their own needs. Alternative sources for providing expertise have emerged and will continue to emerge. In fact it is precisely because the increasingly complicated economy has led the private sector to accumulate large pockets of expertise, that private for-profit providers of information and expertise have emerged to compete with universities in providing the advice and information that is of greatest market value to private organizations. Declines in the cost of transmitting information may first be exploited by these alternative or commercial providers; at that point universities will find themselves in a new competitive environment that will be both challenging and invigorating.

If we use the past to predict the future, the only thing that is clear is that the research university will continue to evolve. Success in the evolutionary struggle requires adaptability. Successful modern research universities attained their current ranking by being adaptable in the past. The rankings of the future will in part be determined by seeing which universities still have the capacity to evolve and which ones don't.

Bibliography

Boyer, Ernest L. *Scholarship Reconsidered: Priorities of the Professoriate.* Princeton: Carnegie Foundation, 1990.

Devon, Tonya K., and Rustum Roy. *Knowledge and Technology Transfer in Wisconsin: Linkages Between Universities and Industry.* Wisconsin Policy Research Institute Report 3, no. 6, November 1990.

Connor, Robert W. "The Future of the American University," in *The Modern University: Its Present Status & Future Prospects*, 65–76. Chapel Hill: William Rand Kenan Jr. Charitable Trust, Chapel Hill, 1994.

Frank, Robert H., and Philip J. Cook. *The Winner-Take-All Society.* New York: Free Press, 1995.

Henderson, Rebecca, Adam B. Jaffe, and Manuel Trajtenberg. "Universities as a Source of Commercial Technology: A Detailed Analysis of University Patenting, 1965–1988." *Review of Economics and Statistics* 80, no. 1 (February 1998) : 119–27.

Horowitz, Helen Lefkowitz. *Campus Life.* New York: Alfred A. Knopf, 1987.

Knox, Alan B., and Joe Corry. "The Wisconsin Idea for the 21st Century," in the Legislative Reference Bureau, *The Wisconsin Blue Book*, 1995–96, pp. 181–93.

Nelson, Richard R., and Nathan Rosenberg. "Technical Innovation and National Systems," in *National Innovation Systems: A Comparative Analysis*, 3–21. New York: Oxford University Press, 1993.

Pappas, James P., ed. "The University's Role in Economic Development: From Research to Outreach." *Directions for Higher Education* 25, no. 1. San Francisco: Jossey Bass, 1997.

Powell, Walter W., and Jason Owen-Smith. "Universities and the Market for Intellectual Property in the Life Sciences." *Journal of Policy Analysis and Management* 17, no. 2 (spring 1998): 253–77.

Stark, Jack. "The Wisconsin Idea: The University's Service to the State," in the Legislative Reference Bureau, *The Wisconsin Blue Book*, 1995–96, pp. 101–80.

Stephan, Paula. "The Economics of Science." *Journal of Economic Literature* 34, no. 3 (September 1996): 1193–1235.

Zilberman, David, Charles Yarkin, and Amir Heiman. "Agricultural Biotechnology: Economic and International Implications." Manuscript, 1998.

A Great Undergraduate University

William Cronon

The Many Meanings of Greatness

It has been commonplace for a very long time now to include the University of Wisconsin–Madison among the small group of American institutions of higher learning that almost always carry the adjective "great" when people across the country and around the world refer to them. More than a century ago, the most famous single sentence in UW history showed no hesitation in asserting the institution's greatness: "Whatever may be the limitations which trammel inquiry elsewhere," wrote the regents in 1894, "we believe that the *great* State University of Wisconsin should ever encourage the continual and fearless sifting and winnowing by which alone the truth can be found." It is of course this historic greatness that we celebrate as we mark the sesquicentennial of the university's founding. But even as we celebrate, it behooves us to think carefully about what exactly we do and do not mean when we apply the adjective "great" to this institution.

The benchmarks of UW–Madison's greatness are not hard to find. Among the crudest is of course sheer size—the large number of students, staff, and faculty members who gather here in their pursuit of knowledge, to say nothing of the buildings and budgets that enable them to do their work—but that is surely not all we

William Cronon is the Frederick Jackson Turner Professor of History, Geography, and Environmental Studies at the University of Wisconsin–Madison. He has directed the L&S Honors Program and is the founding faculty director of Chadbourne Residential College.

mean when we speak of the university's greatness. Another is the tradition we celebrate as the Wisconsin Idea, the notion that the university has a special mission to serve the people of the larger commonweal that supports it. No less important a marker of greatness is the university's longstanding commitment to academic freedom, for which that remarkable 1894 sentence has long served both as symbol and as bulwark. And then there is the extraordinary record of research, whether in the sciences or the humanities, which has placed the University of Wisconsin–Madison at the forefront of human knowledge and discovery ever since its inception. Indeed, the explosive growth of federal and philanthropic funding in the decades immediately following World War II has meant that the adjective "great" has more and more frequently been partnered with another adjective—"research"—when applied to the University of Wisconsin–Madison and a handful of other institutions such as Harvard, Yale, Stanford, Michigan, Berkeley, and a few others. We now speak of these (as we would not have done in quite the same way a century ago) as "great *research* universities," and we pride ourselves for being included among them. Faculty reward systems, institutional measures of self-worth, national rankings, budgets: all now tend to take their bearings from the greatness of the university's research enterprise. Without question, UW–Madison has become a "great research university."

I am second to none in my respect for UW–Madison's commitment to research, and would not myself choose to be a member of its faculty if it were not a "great research university." Still, the question I would like to explore in this chapter relates to another word that might very well be expected to appear (yet rarely does) between the words "great" and "university" in describing this institution and its closest kin. That word is "undergraduate." Is UW–Madison a "great *undergraduate* university"? Even to ask the question is to recognize that this is not the usual way we think of the place: the phrase feels unfamiliar, a little jarring and odd. We're not even quite sure what exactly "a great undergraduate university" is supposed to mean. And therein lies the nub of a crucial challenge, one that will shape the future not just of UW–Madison, but of all research universities in the twenty-first century.

The tendency to define institutional "greatness" without much reference to undergraduate education is a phenomenon by no means limited to UW–Madison. It applies to many of the nation's most distinguished research universities, especially those in the public sector that experienced extraordinary shifts in scale during the post-Sputnik era as their budgets, their physical facilities, their student populations, and their research staffs enjoyed unparalleled growth with the hitherto unheard-of influx of federal and foundation funding. Institutions and faculties that had formerly counted undergraduate teaching among their most important tasks gradually came to see this role as secondary or even tertiary behind professorial research and graduate training. (This shift was most pronounced in the natural and social sciences, but in fact affected all disciplines.) As a result, many seem to have forgotten how much the university's past greatness—and, I would argue, its future greatness as well—are inextricably tied to the excellence of the education it offers its most junior members. If great state universities are to prosper in the decades ahead, we can afford to forget neither this most basic mission, nor the social compact between these institutions and the taxpayers, parents, and students who provide such a large share of the funding that enables research universities to exist.

For me, the most vivid example of how easy it has become to lose track of this social compact is a local one, though parallels would be easy to find at universities across the country. The broader academic culture that this anecdote reflects belongs not just to UW–Madison, but to American higher education at the close of the twentieth century. In the fall of 1995, Dean Phillip Certain released a visionary report entitled *Creating a New College*, itself a response to Chancellor David Ward's mission statement describing the university as a "learning community." In his report, Dean Certain declared that the UW's College of Letters and Science should renew its historic commitment to undergraduate education by significantly improving the quality of its teaching for baccalaureate students. Perhaps surprisingly, the general response to this recommendation on the part of many faculty members bordered on outrage. Many evidently regarded the dean's proposals as misplaced or inappropriate for an institution of UW–Madison's high stature and "greatness." When professors explained their reasons for resisting the report's proposed reforms, they repeated a single sentence as if it were a self-evident refutation of Dean Certain's emphasis on undergraduates: "But this," they said, "is a *research* university!"

The particulars of this old controversy need not concern us here. Dean Certain's report undoubtedly had weaknesses, and faculty members undoubtedly had good reasons to criticize those weaknesses. I do not mean to caricature either side of the debate. But what I nonetheless find both intriguing and suggestive is the ease with which so many professors resorted to the assertion "But this is a *research* university!" to argue against a recommendation that they should devote more time, more energy, and greater care to undergraduate teaching. Implicit in that reaction was a host of assumptions about the university's different missions and their relative importance. Implicit too were deeply held beliefs about institutional greatness, since many faculty members were evidently convinced that a great research university must necessarily be less committed than other schools to undergraduate education.

No one argued against good teaching. No one defended faculty members who ignore their undergraduates. No one denied that the university owes its students a good education. But, curiously enough, few participants in this debate seemed inclined to believe that Dean Certain and his critics might *both* be right: that the university should hold itself to the highest possible standards in *both* realms, teaching no less than research. UW–Madison might be a fine place to earn a baccalaureate, but the controversy surrounding Certain's report suggested that this was not where many faculty members looked when defining the university's true "greatness." That prize lay elsewhere, in the laboratories and archives that few undergraduates ever experience at first hand.

Why Even Research Universities Should Care About Undergraduates

My goal in this chapter is to argue on behalf of the middle ground: not *against* great research, but *for* great teaching. I believe that the two are far more complementary, and far more essential to any viable definition of a great university, than the academic culture of the past half-century has typically affirmed. Furthermore, I hold that the familiar dichotomy between research and teaching is not only unnecessary and misleading, but actually threatens the mission and long-term survival even of elite universities that are most deeply committed to their research enterprise. This perceived dichotomy is hardly unique to the University of Wisconsin–Madison; it affects all research universities to at least some degree. The challenge these institutions will face in the tumultuous and often hostile fiscal and political environment of the new century is to reinvigorate their teaching without undermining what is best in their research.

No one should be in doubt about the reality of the hostile environment universities now face. The past two decades have seen the most far-reaching criticisms of American higher education since the McCarthyite days of the Cold War. Some of the most visible attacks have been nakedly ideological, with culture wars and accusations of political correctness adding new vitriol to longstanding campus battles between the Left and the Right. The culture wars have generated well-funded groups and critics with an interest in fueling public doubts about supposedly left-leaning universities, and these have been remarkably effective in attracting media attention to themselves. For tactical reasons, their attacks have not always focused overtly on politics. And so the research/teaching dichotomy has proven to be a convenient weapon: portrayals of faculty members pursuing politically obnoxious and/or trivial research at the expense of their students make for good copy, sell publications, and provide grist for the radio talk-show mills.

But ideological warfare is too easy a scapegoat to explain the situation in which academia now finds itself. More important and more worrisome are numerous calls for greater accountability on the part of colleges and universities, and a widespread perception that these institutions are as arrogant, wasteful, insular, and self-serving as other large organizations that are held in equally low regard by the public. Reflecting the generalized post-Watergate suspicion of once-respected professions and institutions, these calls for accountability have usually been regarded within the academy more as irritating annoyances than as fundamental threats. Few academics seriously entertain the thought that greater accountability might legitimately be warranted—no doubt because they share with other Americans the same suspicions of the arrogant, wasteful, insular, and self-serving institutions that would do the accounting. (Sauce for the goose is sauce for the gander.)

Responding to such criticisms, faculty and staff members at Wisconsin and elsewhere have begun to develop new teaching initiatives and new undergraduate programs that demonstrate their commitment to students. But the underlying postwar academic culture in which prestige, salary, and other rewards flow almost entirely toward research has been very slow to change. The disconnect between internal and external perceptions of the university's mission thus persists, as do the perils associated with it. Most members of the public continue to believe that what they are primarily buying from universities with their tax dollars and tuition payments is education—and education primarily for undergraduates. In contrast, most faculty members who work in the "great universities" believe that their most valuable and distinguished product, the one on which their personal reputations chiefly rest, is research. Mutual confusion, frustration, and suspicions about inadequate accountability can hardly help but surface in such an environment, with all sorts of dangerous political and fiscal consequences.

One obvious response is for universities to do a much better job of explaining their research activities to a public that too often experiences academic inquiry as opaque and incomprehensible at best, trivial and self-indulgent at worst. Certainly this work of explanation and translation needs to be done, and researchers would do well to tackle it at the most fundamental level. They need to ask not just how they can help the public better understand what they do, but also how their research will make the kind of difference out there in the world that the public might actually care about. If this sounds easy, it is only because academia too often assumes that the answers to such questions are self-evident. They are not.

I will soon argue that one of the best available places for confronting hard questions of this sort is precisely the undergraduate classroom, but for now I want to turn to the other half of the case universities must mount on their own behalf. Yes, absolutely, they must respond to the current political and fiscal environment by defending their research enterprise as passionately and persuasively as they can. But they must also articulate with equal conviction the strength of their commitment to undergraduate education. Here the audience that universities like Wisconsin must persuade is not just a doubting public, but their own students and faculties, who have accumulated many years' worth of good hard evidence that undergraduate teaching is not taken nearly so seriously or rewarded nearly so highly as cutting-edge research.

How does one make a case against such evidence? How does one persuade a research-oriented professoriate to recognize the absolute centrality of undergraduate teaching to the mission of a great university?

One could start with rather crass arguments. Even if one has only the most self-interested reasons for making sure that a place like Wisconsin can honestly claim to be a "great undergraduate university," self-interested reasons can still be pretty compelling. Here are a few that spring to mind.

Undergraduates are the main reason taxpayers and parents support the university. Because professors know that the national fame of their departments (and therefore, by extension, their own reputations) depends on how other academics view the quality of their research and the stature of their graduate programs, they too easily forget that such fame is not the main reason that the taxpayers of Wisconsin and other states (to say nothing of the nation as a whole) support institutions like UW–Madison. Neither is it the main reason that students and their parents pay tuition bills. The extraordinary public good will that American colleges and universities have long enjoyed has flowed first and foremost from a powerful commitment especially on the part of parents, but more generally society as a whole, to provide the best possible education to much-loved children as they leave home and stand on the threshold of adulthood. To raise doubts in the minds of parents and citizens about whether research universities share this powerful, almost sacred intergenerational commitment is perilous indeed—even, one might say, suicidal. Yet this is precisely what an overriding commitment to excellence in research conveys unless it is always coupled with an equally stalwart commitment to excellence in teaching.

It is easy to assert that Wisconsin's best undergraduates benefit from attending a world-class research university. It is harder to prove that the institution consistently makes good on this claim. I would not for a moment deny that UW–Madison has made great strides in improving undergraduate advising and teaching over the past decade, and there are certainly statistics that can demonstrate this. But the questions I have in mind about the place of undergraduates in a research university run deeper, and are not so easily answered with mere statistics. They have to do with the intimate human relationships that lie at the heart of teaching and learning, the caring and nurturing and mentoring that happen when students find themselves in a place that really challenges and helps them grow. Are we confident that most UW–Madison undergraduates gain as much as we would hope from attending this great research university? Are faculty and staff members confident enough of their answer to this question that they would unhesitatingly send their own child to UW–Madison if money were no object and they had complete freedom to choose the school that would give their child the best possible undergraduate experience? And what might the university do to assure that the preponderant answer to both these questions will be "yes"? I offer these questions *not* as implied criticisms of UW–Madison, but as moral touchstones to which all colleges and universities must perennially return if they are to fulfill their own highest ideals. Although no legislative audit will ever do justice to them, *these* are the criteria by which a great undergraduate university must hold itself accountable.

Improving undergraduate education at UW–Madison and other research universities requires an honest recognition that not all criticisms of such places—about the ways in which faculty research and graduate education can sometimes detract from undergraduate teaching—are without merit. If universities want parents and other citizens to keep supporting the work they do, they must make absolutely certain that they do the best possible job of delivering the core services—teaching and mentoring beloved children into adulthood—that parents and citizens so earnestly desire. As an alumnus of this university who feels nothing but the deepest gratitude for the education I received from UW–Madison, my own conviction is that a great research university can offer as good an undergraduate education as any institution on the planet . . . but it will fail to deliver this unless it places undergraduate teaching at the heart of its mission. And if it fails to do so, it will have only itself to blame when disappointed taxpayers and parents decide to send their money elsewhere.

Undergraduates soon become the alumni who play an indispensable role in supporting the long-term health of UW–Madison. It has long been true that the private liberal arts colleges of the United States have done a better job than other institutions of upholding the core values of liberal education and undergraduate teaching, but even the great private research universities seem generally to be more attentive to their undergraduates than the great public research universities. Places like Princeton or Yale or Stanford go to extraordinary lengths to make sure their students feel great satisfaction with the education they receive, far more so than at places like Berkeley or Michigan or Wisconsin. Although this may seem paradoxical, given the tradition of outreach and service that is so central to public institutions like UW–Madison, there are good practical reasons for the phenomenon.

One reason involves the sheer number of students that the public universities serve. It is much harder to make 25,000 undergraduates feel that each one of them is a special individual with special talents and special needs, or that they belong to a special community and are receiving a special educational experience, than it is to do the same for 1,000 or 5,000 or even 10,000. Quite apart from this problem of scale, there are good financial reasons as well for the different ways private and public institutions regard their students. When undergraduate tuition soars to the levels it does at the private schools, each individual undergraduate, on a per capita basis, represents a much more significant share of the institutional income stream. It takes just two or three undergraduate tuitions to pay an assistant professor's salary at an elite private school; it takes many times that number to do the same at a place like Wisconsin.

Most importantly, private universities for a very long time have understood much better than public ones that happy undergraduates become loyal alumni, and loyal alumni become the benefactors who underwrite a university's future greatness. As every development officer has good reason to know, the bulk of alumni gifts come more frequently from former undergraduates than from former graduate students. If one is interested in cultivating future philanthropic giving, it would be foolish indeed to emphasize one's commitment to graduate students at the expense of undergraduates. Even if a university were completely indifferent to the nobler goals of undergraduate education, it would be extraordinarily short-sighted to forego the task of nurturing this future income stream. Yet this is precisely what public universities have tended to do, at least when compared with their private counterparts.

And there is still one more angle to consider. As a state university, most of UW–Madison's future alumni will become future state taxpayers (to say nothing of those who end up as future legislators and governors!). Even if alumni choose not to make private gifts of their own, their view of their alma mater will crucially affect their behavior in the voting booth. It is alumni—former undergraduates—who will tell other citizens of the state whether they think the university is being a good steward of the money (and the young adults) that comes its way. When professors complain about legislators who speak ill of UW–Madison in the State Capitol, they should perhaps consider whether those criticisms arise from first-hand experience of what it means to be a student at this school. By being anything less than a great undergraduate university, UW–Madison runs the risk not just of failing to nurture alumni donations but also of undermining its future support from taxpayers. No one should be under any illusions about how dangerous this would be to the university's long-term health and prosperity. If for no other reason than to sustain its research enterprise, UW–Madison cannot afford to be anything less than a great undergraduate university. A chief lesson to learn from private institutions is the importance of treating current undergraduates as future alumni, with the respect and gratitude that both groups deserve for the many generous ways they support the university.

Even if the one institutional goal were only to train graduate students, helping them become first-rate undergraduate teachers is central to that goal. However important undergraduates may be to the university's political and economic health, some faculty members will nonetheless continue to regard graduate teaching as their most important pedagogy. Having committed oneself to the deep, rigorous knowledge of a particular discipline, it's easy to imagine that one's most important task is to pass on this knowledge to students who are equally committed to the discipline. (Never mind the obvious point that graduate students began their careers as undergraduates and presumably came to their calling because some great teacher helped motivate them to go deeper into the subject.) A different kind of instrumental logic on behalf of undergraduates may prove more persuasive for those who focus mainly on graduate students. Doctoral students who will ultimately be successful in securing employment in their own disciplines, will, for the most part, obtain jobs in which they are primarily paid to *teach*. Unless they have had the experience of doing first-rate undergraduate teaching while attending graduate school, and have watched and learned from faculty members who regard this as one of the most important missions (along *with* research) of their professional life, graduate students will not learn to be the kind of teachers that other institutions will want to hire. And so, ironically, the stature of a university's graduate programs can suffer from the weakness in its undergraduate ones.

Paying graduate students to serve as teaching assistants is not by itself enough to assure that they are receiving first-rate preparation as undergraduate teachers. At too many institutions, professors regard teaching assistants as an excuse for not having to waste their time on the nitty-gritty details of designing syllabi, leading discussion sections, writing exams, making thoughtful criticisms, grading fairly, and having real face-to-face relationships with undergraduates other than from behind a podium. If graduate students are to learn how to teach, they must witness great teaching at first hand, from faculty members who deliver great lectures but who also design great syllabi, lead great discussion sections, prepare great exams and paper assignments, and serve as great mentors. By constantly displaying their own deep commitment to undergraduate teaching, professors can demonstrate the skills and techniques that will prepare graduate students for the jobs they will soon be competing to secure. An institution that fails to prepare graduate students to be great undergraduate teachers in this way fails willy-nilly to deliver the world-class *graduate* training on which its own reputation in part depends. Its Ph.D.'s eventually stop obtaining jobs at the best colleges and universities in the country, and the university's own reputation and stature decline accordingly. If UW–Madison wishes to avoid such a fate, it must make sure that it keeps its graduate programs in constant dialogue with its undergraduate ones.

Higher Truths

Convincing as they may be, these self-serving, instrumental reasons for making sure that a great university offers its undergraduates the best possible educational experience are not finally the most persuasive ones. In fact, undergraduate teaching is every bit as important as research to the mission even of a research university, because without the ability to interpret, translate, and communicate what they do, the work of scholars and scientists remains inert and of little value to anyone but themselves. If this is so, then one can make additional arguments on behalf of undergraduate teaching that are all the more compelling because they speak to the university's highest ideals.

Undergraduates are the university's best protection against forgetting how its work relates to the larger public. There is much talk these days about the decline of the public intellectual, about the isolation of the academy from civic life. There cannot be much question that the growing specialization of the academic disciplines, for all the intellectual power this process has generated, has had the unfortunate consequence of isolating academic intellectuals from the larger realm of public discourse. Indeed, it has made it hard for professors even to understand *each other's* work, let alone communicate the meaning of what they do to members of the public who are mystified about whether academic work has any larger value.

How do we reverse this trend? How do those inside the academy learn to communicate more effectively with members of the general public? My own answer is that professors need constantly to remember that they meet the public every day in their classrooms. There is no better way to learn how to communicate one's ideas in forceful, compelling, ordinary English prose than to try to persuade bright undergraduates that those ideas are not only important, but fascinating. If all faculty members regarded their undergraduate classrooms as the place where they learn how to talk and write about their work in ways that make it accessible and even exciting to a wider audience, not only would their teaching improve, but so would their writing and public outreach. This, surely, is what the Wisconsin Idea is supposed to be all about.

Learning how to translate the arcane knowledge of an academic discipline into the realm of public discourse is uniquely a benefit (and a benefit for far more than just professors) that flows from first-rate undergraduate teaching. Graduate students, who have already committed themselves to the disciplinary identity of their faculty mentors, by definition are already aspiring to learn the difficult private languages of the academy: they desire to speak those languages for themselves, not to have them be translated and rendered more accessible. Because undergraduates have not made a comparable commitment, they are always asking to be persuaded that the material they are learning is really worthwhile—a challenge any good teacher must always be prepared to meet with energy and passion. Bright, curious, doubting sophomores are far better surrogates than their older peers for the "lay" audiences that academic intellectuals are forever tempted to forget or ignore, albeit at their own peril. Without undergraduates, professors too easily forget how to talk with anyone but themselves.

Far more so than in research or graduate teaching, the undergraduate curriculum is where the work of disciplinary synthesis occurs. What happens in the undergraduate classroom is not just the translation of complex ideas and arcane vocabularies into ordinary language. Rather, the undergraduate curriculum forces disciplinary specialists to grapple with what their own disciplines constantly encourage them to evade: the profound question of how the diverse intellectual perspectives of the modern academy come together to produce a coherent (or at least richly complex and interconnected) view of the world and of the human experience within it. Undergraduate teaching, if done right, is where research scholars and scientists cannot avoid the tasks of synthesis and integration that are essential counterpoints to the analysis and specialization that ordinarily typify the research enterprise.

Too often, universities rely on a menu of curricular requirements, forcing students to take a diverse set of courses, which, when combined together, will supposedly yield a broad general education. Faculty members rarely bother to ask whether they themselves could integrate knowledge across the intellectual terrain they are forcing their students to navigate. It is hard to imagine the modern college curriculum without distributional requirements, but by themselves these are a sorry substitute for the far more difficult task of trying to find the common ground, for instance, among such achievements of the modern academy as the deciphering of Linear B, the discovery of plate tectonics, the DNA sequencing of the human genome, the critical exegesis of Emily Dickinson or James Joyce or Toni Morrison, and the management of modern economies via the manipulation of interest rates by central banks. Undergraduates are asked to take courses on subjects such as these all the time, but how often are they or their teachers asked to make sense of the interstices that lie in between? Is the extraordinary storehouse of understanding and knowledge that constitutes the modern university more than just the sum of its parts? Do faculty and staff members offer their students a coherent or unified or integrated view of what the *uni*-versity as a whole has to offer?

No one, surely, has definitive answers to questions like these, but that is no reason they shouldn't be asked, over and over again. And the fact that such questions are by their nature rather "sophomoric" is precisely their value: it is sophomores who force experts to keep returning to first principles to ask "Big Questions." Experts are surely the better for having to do so. One of the chief benefits of sophomoric "Big Questions" is that sooner or later they always circle back to questions of value and meaning about how parts relate to a greater whole. Along the way, they remind one that mere technical expertise is rarely enough to supply the passionate caring that can turn mere "disciplines" or "subjects" into profoundly moving ways of engaging the world. And this in turn teaches one final lesson which is very near the heart of what a great university should finally be all about.

More than anywhere else, the undergraduate classroom is where students and teachers come together to reaffirm and transmit from one generation to the next the love of learning and the life of the mind. If working closely with undergraduates can keep reminding professors of the need for translation and synthesis and the sharing of intellectual passion, it can transform not just students but teachers as well. It reminds scholars and scientists as few other activities do why and how their work matters out in the larger world. The greatest joy of undergraduate teaching is in watching the profound acts of human discovery—the dawning of new perspectives and new insights and new ideas—that happen over and over again in the classroom. Witnessing this and serving as this kind of catalyst for moments of undergraduate discovery is one of the greatest privileges of working at a college or university. But to fully appreciate the power of this role, professors must choose to be present for it, and too many faculty members don't allow themselves the time or the energy or the direct involvement with undergraduates even to notice the kind of catalyst—welcoming or forbidding, stimulating or stultifying, sought-after or avoided, beloved or despised—that they could become for the young people they serve.

In conversations with colleagues at Wisconsin and elsewhere, I have been struck by the number of senior professors who, after long years of being committed first and foremost to their own research productivity, become newly engaged with undergraduates (and critical of their own earlier relative inattention to these most junior of the university's students) as they send their own children off to college. Now finding themselves vicariously at the receiving end of the university's pedagogy, they suddenly gain a view of the classroom from the opposite side of the lectern, and what they see is not always flattering. Having believed that the primary measure of a university's "greatness" was its research, they now recognize with some surprise that this is not what they themselves care most about for their own children: what they want is a great *undergraduate* university or college. Although one might cynically regard this as a case of yuppie parents selfishly seeking the best for their own, in fact I've seen such parents throw themselves into the classroom with a will and an energy that they had not always brought to their teaching before. What I see them trying to share is not just their technical expertise, but their passion, their commitment to the life of the mind, and their desire to help young people who are much like their own children discover these things for themselves. Any institution that can sustain a culture in which professors regard the love of learning as the single most important gift they pass along to their students (a gift they would want their own children to possess) can be pretty confident that its greatness will not be limited merely to what goes on in the archive or the laboratory.

One small step in this direction might be to mandate that every faculty member not just teach undergraduates in big lecture courses, but lead undergraduate seminars and discussion sections (and direct senior theses) as well. Teaching assistants should not be the only academics who regularly meet in small-group settings with freshmen and sophomores. Even a reform as seemingly trivial and mechanical as this would mean that every professor could get to know at least a few undergraduates by name, and that every student could interact in a more personal way with at least a few senior faculty members, thereby encouraging the kinds of human relationships that only happen when people know each other's names. (For much the same reason, there is a lot to be said for having administrators continue to teach small undergraduate classes as a way to experience the concrete effects of university policies at first hand.) This may feel like extra work—an incremental teaching load beyond the burden professors and administrators think they should have to bear—but the benefits not just to teaching but to research and outreach are so great that in fact the time could hardly be better spent. Giving up a few extra committee meetings in return for encouraging a few more interactions between undergraduates and faculty members can hardly hurt the university. For it is in the resulting conversations—not lectures, but *conversations*—that students and professors come to know each other well enough to learn at first hand the ways in which a great research university can also be—*must* also be—a great undergraduate university.

What a Great Undergraduate University Teaches

What are the characteristics we would expect to find in a "great undergraduate university"? How do we know whether a research university deserves to be called "great" in the eyes of its undergraduates?

Most simply, a great undergraduate university is a place where everyone—faculty, staff, and students—understands that teaching is at the absolute core of the university's mission; where teaching is viewed not as a distraction from the "real" work of research, but as an essential complement to it. Such a university works to make sure that faculty members never lose sight of the intimate linkage between research and teaching. This is far from an easy task, because the professional culture and narrow self-interests of faculty members too often seem to point *away* from the classroom. It takes a self-conscious commitment on the part of the institution as a whole to make sure professors are regularly brought back into dialogue with undergraduates, not as an obligation but as a high calling that the university itself both celebrates and rewards. Individual professors inevitably see their disciplines and their own research as ends in themselves requiring no further defense or justification, and this, curiously, can be an important source of trouble in the classroom. If teachers assume that their own subjects are already fascinating, if they fail to see that one of their primary tasks is to persuade students to fall in love with those subjects, then the classrooms in which they work are unlikely ever to come alive. A university whose culture genuinely nurtures first-rate teaching regularly reminds faculty members that, from an undergraduate's point of view, they and their disciplines are almost always a means to other ends, rarely ends in themselves. Everything about professors—who they are, what they most care about, and why they do what they do—tempts them to forget this fundamental fact, thereby undermining their effectiveness as teachers.

Certainly, professors teach undergraduates arcane knowledge and technical skills, and good teachers struggle to do this as well as they can. But good teachers also never lose track of the much deeper lessons about life and the world that lie far beneath the surface of even the most essential information. It is these deeper lessons that students are most likely to remember in the long run, and I would include among them the following:

- How to care passionately about ideas, both one's own and those of other people;
- How to follow and make logical arguments;
- How to recognize rigor, probing always to test for false assumptions and biases;
- How to write;
- How to talk;

- How to navigate the world of numbers;
- How to watch and learn from the world as scientists and poets do;
- How to gain from other people's diverse experiences, talents, and passions;
- How to make friends who are very different from oneself;
- How to practice tolerance while still articulating and defending one's own beliefs;
- How to dream adult dreams, imagining and working toward the goal of a fulfilled adult life;
- How to empower oneself and one's community;
- How to get things done and make a difference in the world.

Any institution that succeeds in teaching such lessons to even a sizable fraction of its students is a great undergraduate university indeed, benefiting not just its students and itself, but the larger community it serves. These deeper lessons of undergraduate education are conveyed as much by the *way* professors teach, the *way* they share their lives and passions with students, as by the substantive content of their courses. I hasten to add that the substantive content of courses hardly plays a trivial or unimportant role, for the paradox of these deep life lessons, if they are to be truly learned and earned, is that they can only be taught indirectly, via a rigorous encounter with a substance and discipline that resist the callow assumptions of an untrained sophomoric mind. And the "love of learning" that a great teacher shares is not an abstract love, but a deeply committed passion for a very particular body of knowledge and inquiry, more often than not acquired in the practice of doing research. The content of the course, the content of the curriculum, the pedagogical expression of the research enterprise: these are absolutely crucial. And yet—this is the other half of the paradox—I'm also convinced that most of the information undergraduates learn in their classes vanishes from memory within a few weeks, a few months, a few years. If professors had to justify their salaries on the basis of how many students could pass a detailed examination on the content of their classes twenty or thirty years after graduation, few professors would stay employed for long. But if those courses were taught well, if the teacher really connected with the students and shared something profound in the time they spent together, then there need be no fear that the deeper lessons will fail to last a lifetime. Once learned, they will not soon be forgotten.

This is why universities must work to sustain a culture in which professors regularly ask themselves whether their teaching actually delivers what students most need to learn. If their particular course were the only chance professors had to pass on to their own children not just the content of a discipline but an understanding of how that discipline connects to the world and to a life well lived, what would the resulting course look like? A course designed in response to such a question is bound to look rather different from one in which formal disciplinary content is the teacher's sole concern, and professors fool themselves if they don't know in their hearts which kind of course students would prefer to take. Indeed, one has only to think back on the courses one most remembers from one's own undergraduate years to know what it takes to leave a lasting mark on students. Good teachers from time to time revisit in their memory those cherished classes of long ago—revisit them in gratitude and wonder—to remind themselves of the kinds of legacies that a great class, a great teacher, a great university can leave.

If we remember that *these* are our goals—that *these* are the most basic things we teach—then there are few better places than a research university for undergraduates to acquire an education. There are, after all, few more passionate realms in which the life of the mind intersects with the broader life of the world than in research (broadly understood as the struggle to make sense of the world), whether this entails understanding the inner architecture of matter, the history of life on earth, or the moral struggle for human justice. If the university strives constantly to share its research enterprise with undergraduates (whether by bringing faculty research experience into the classroom or by drawing undergraduates into doing research themselves, as UW–Madison has done so successfully with its senior honors theses and Hilldale Fellowships) it will be giving those students something quite irreplaceable. The pedagogical value of research arises *not* because students will go on to be academic researchers—most of course will not—but because this kind of engagement in fact translates into virtually every imaginable walk of life, whether in law or medicine or farming or art or public policy or community organizing.

To repeat: my own deepest faith is that no university can be truly great if it sees research as its only or most crucial mission. Unless universities couple the rigor and depth of their research enterprise with the breadth and delight that come from great undergraduate teaching, they will not only fail to defend themselves against those who believe they aren't doing the work they are paid to do . . . they will in fact betray their own best vision of what an institution of higher learning should be. The task of universities is not just to discover knowledge. It is also to translate and share that knowledge so that everyone—freshman and sophomores and members of the public as well as faculty colleagues and graduate students—can understand and appreciate its importance and power. Moreover, if professors fail in their teaching to inspire undergraduates in the same ways that they themselves were inspired to pursue the vision of excellence that has shaped their own adult lives, if they fall short in this task of inspiration, then at some very deep level they will be leaving the most important work of a great university to someone else.

And so this is why I find myself hoping for a different rejoinder the next time a debate occurs (whether at Wisconsin or elsewhere) in which someone responds to calls for improved undergraduate education by saying, "But this is a *research* university!" I hope students and teachers will leap into the fray by insisting with equal conviction: "But it must also be a great *undergraduate* university!" Because unless both of these statements are true, and true in equal measure, no university can be truly great.